# JOHN
# LOCKE

# JOHN LOCKE

## Economist and Social Scientist

### KAREN IVERSEN VAUGHN

The
University of Chicago
Press

The University of Chicago Press, Chicago 60637
The Althone Press, London
© 1980 by The University of Chicago
All rights reserved. Published 1980
Paperback edition 1982
Printed in the United States of America
87  86  85  84  83  82    5  4  3  2


LIBRARY OF CONGRESS CATALOGING IN PUBLICATION DATA

Vaughn, Karen I
  John Locke, economist and social scientist.

  Bibliography: p.
  Includes index.
  1. Locke, John, 1632–1704—Economics.  I. Title.
HB103.L6V38      330.1      79-17875
ISBN: 0-226-85166-4 (cloth)
      0-226-85167-2 (paper)

To my first teacher, Josef Soudek,
with gratitude and affection.

# CONTENTS

# PREFACE

If one were to go into the reference room of any major library and open the card catalogue to *Locke, John (1632–1704)*, one would find listed, in addition to multiple editions of all of Locke's works, scores of books devoted to analyzing his contributions to philosophy, political theory, education, theology, ideas on toleration, and even medicine. What one would not find among all these references would be a single book or monograph in English devoted to analyzing Locke's contributions to economics, in spite of the fact that he was a recognized authority on economic problems in his own time and an influential figure in later economic thought. This omission would be amazing in any other field, but economics is a discipline which more and more relies on the journals to communicate its research. A perusal of the American Economic Association Index for the last eighty years, however, will turn up only one article devoted to John Locke's contribution to economic science.

This is not to say that Locke has been entirely neglected by the historians of economic thought. There have been several excellent discussions of aspects of his economic ideas, specifically William Letwin's chapter on Locke in his *The Origins of Scientific Economics,* and Douglas Vickers's treatment of

Locke's monetary theories in his *Studies in the Theory of Money, 1690–1776*. In addition, the relationship of Locke's economics to his political philosophy was the subject of chapter 5 of James Bonar's *Philosophy and Political Economy,* while the relationship between Locke's epistemology and his economic theories was the subject of the first essay in Werner Stark's *The Ideal Foundations of Economic Thought.* Locke is mentioned in most books that deal with seventeenth-century economic theories, and almost all textbooks in the history of economic doctrines give him at least a nod. In addition, Locke's monetary theory has recently been the subject of an article by Arthur H. Leigh, "John Locke and the Quantity Theory of Money," in *History of Political Economy.* But while there is plenty of evidence available that Locke was an important figure in the seventeenth century who also was concerned with some economic problems, there is little evidence that he was an important figure in economics. No one as yet has undertaken to present a comprehensive treatment of John Locke's position in the development of economic thought.

The following work is an attempt to provide such a treatment. I have tried to present a detailed exposition and analysis of Locke's economic theories and, more specifically, his theory of value, which I believe he used as a model for his discussion of all other economic variables. Also, I have tried to establish the influences on his thought, his relationship to his contemporaries, and the connection between his economic theory and his theory of political society. This last, I believe, represents the core of Locke's economic and social ideas and was the basis for much eighteenth-century social theory.

My efforts fall short of a complete treatment of Locke in the following ways. I have made no attempt to systematically analyze Locke's role in policy formation, except insofar as it illustrates his theoretical conclusions. This could be a fertile area for further study, considering the long association with

Shaftesbury of Locke's middle years and his tenure on the Board of Trade late in his life. Nor have I tried to tackle the problem of establishing the authenticity of the text of Locke's essays now in use, or dealt with the circulation of the essays after their publication. Professor Patrick Kelly of the University of Dublin is now engaged in preparing a definitive edition of Locke's economic essays, so we will have to wait for the publication of his work to be enlightened on these issues.

Finally, I have made little attempt in the following pages to assess the influence Locke had on later economic thought. It is well known that in France Richard Cantillon read Locke's essays before writing his own *Essai sur la nature du commerce en général* between 1730 and 1734, and that Adam Smith in Scotland referred to them in *The Wealth of Nations*. Further, Ferdinando Galiani is reputed to have introduced himself to economics by translating Locke's first essay and, in general, Locke's work was well known in Italy. However, very little is actually known about the influence Locke's economic writings had on these eighteenth-century economists, or if his work was read at all by many others. It would be interesting to discover the extent to which Locke's economics had an impact on the development of economic thought in the eighteenth century, but that would be to study how eighteenth-century economists interpreted Locke more than what Locke himself had to say.

What I have found during the course of my research is that Locke was a far more sophisticated economist than most historians of economic thought have given him credit for being. Also, my examination of his political writings for their economic implications has convinced me that Locke was in many respects an early social scientist with a consistent view of social action in both his economic and political writings, a claim that may to some seem equally controversial. For while no one doubts that Locke was an economist of sorts, and few would quarrel that his political writings make a seminal contribution to political philosophy, no one to my knowledge has suggested that he be considered an early social scientist. Letwin included Locke in the group of writers who originated scientific economics, but said nothing specific about social science. Schumpeter included Locke in his group of Protestant Scholastics who he claimed were all following the Scholastic tradition of creating a unified science of man, but specifically excluded Locke's economics. It is a major concern of this work to show that if one defines social science in a manner that is by no means excessively broad—as an attempt to explain human social interaction in a systematic way, based on assumptions about the characteristics of individual human beings—Locke's writings on economics and politics fit this definition.

Having said this, I now want to emphasize that I do not suggest here that Locke was an anticipator of everything modern. He was a brilliant man living in an intellectually stimulating time, but one cannot hope to find in his works all of modern economic and political theory in embryonic form. Neither do I hope to show that Locke consciously set out to construct a unified theory of social interaction, since the actual circumstances of his writing suggest exactly the opposite. What I do find, however, is that although Locke's economic and political theories were responses to current social problems, his scholarly mind and his lifelong intellectual habits were such that a unity of thought is present in his writings on these current issues. Furthermore, and more to the point of this study, the unity of thought which is characteristic of his work is of a basically scientific and objective nature.

# ACKNOWLEDGMENTS

Although any errors to be found in the following pages are my own, what there is of merit is due largely to the generous help I have received. Financially, my work was supported over the years by a grant from the Committee on International Studies at Duke University which permitted me to do research at the Bodleian Library, Oxford, during the summer of 1969, by a faculty research grant from the University of Tennessee during the summer of 1972, and by a postdoctoral fellowship from the Institute for Humane Studies for the summer of 1975.

Although financial aid was important to the completion of this book, it is overshadowed in significance by the generous substantive help which I have received from colleagues and friends. Professor Joseph J. Spengler, Duke University, provided me with a great deal of help on earlier drafts of this work and continued to encourage me to complete it. Professor Josef Soudek, Queens College, CUNY, first suggested the topic of Locke's economics to me as a possible area of study and has continued to show his interest in my project by giving me many valuable suggestions especially with regard to Locke's value theory. Professor Laurence Moss, Babson College, has read drafts of several chapters and has always helped me to clarify my meaning in passages that otherwise would have remained obscure. Professor William Letwin, University College, London, provided me with detailed comments on chapter 2 and thereby helped me to clear up some disturbing confusions in my analysis. What confusions remain are doubtless due to the fact that I did not always follow his recommendations. Professor Patrick Kelly, University of Dublin, read several earlier drafts of this work and gave me the benefit of his vast knowledge of Locke by correcting some historical and scholarly errors. He also helped me greatly by permitting me to read his introduction to *Locke on Money* in typescript.

Finally, I want to thank Mrs. Sue Cooper for fast, efficient, and cheerful typing services, and the Economics Department at George Mason University for providing the funds to enable me to benefit from Mrs. Cooper's speed, efficiency, and good cheer.

K. I. V.

# ONE

# Introduction

## BIOGRAPHY

JOHN LOCKE WAS born in Somerset in 1632 to a moderately well-off family of the minor gentry.[1] His grandfather had been a successful clothier and his father a less successful lawyer. There were two children in the family of which John was the elder. Very little is known of Locke's early childhood other than his own word that his father was strict and remote when he was a child but gradually became more accessible as he got older. Among the more important facts that we do know is that Locke's family were Puritans and that his father fought with the parliamentary army during the Revolution from 1642 to its ultimate victory in 1649. Locke's Puritan background is important primarily because his father, as a result of his service to Cromwell's army, was able to secure for his son the best education England had to offer at that time. After the triumph of Cromwell, Westminster School, one of the most famous and influential public schools in England, fell under the control of the Long Parliament, and it was there that the young Locke, at the age of fifteen, began his formal education.

*Formal* is a more than usually descriptive word for the kind of education being meted out at Westminster in 1647. The

1

school was then headed by the famous Richard Busby, a staunch Royalist who still somehow managed to keep both his position and his integrity throughout the days of the Commonwealth. Busby's idea of a sound education was to provide his charges with thorough training in Latin and Greek with a smattering of Hebrew and Arabic thrown in for good measure. During his five-year stay at Westminster, Locke certainly became proficient in the technique of translating into and out of and composing poetry in the classical languages, if nothing else. Very little time was allocated for anything but study and prayer, and Locke's estimation of this kind of schooling is well illustrated by his later recommendation of a private tutor for all but the most recalcitrant of children.

The real advantage of going to Westminster was that its scholars might try for a place at Christ Church, Oxford, or Trinity College, Cambridge. Locke chose, successfully, to try for the former, and in the autumn of 1652 he entered Oxford, where he remained for the next fifteen years, growing from a sheltered Christ Church scholar of twenty to a fellow and man in search of the larger world at thirty-five. During these fifteen years Locke studied and wrote, but never published a word, and indeed was totally unknown except for his own varied circle of friends. Yet these fifteen years were essential to the formation of his thought and to his future work. It was during this time that he encountered two of the three major influences on his later thoughts on economics.

The Oxford that Locke found when he entered in 1652, decimated as it was by the effects of the Civil War, was far different from the prestigious institution of modern times. During the war it had been a Royalist stronghold, housing the king and queen and their retinue of courtiers and cavaliers as well as most of the royal army. The university had been called on again and again to give support to the king in the form of both money and men, and by the end of hostilities its academic aims had been so totally superseded by the requirements of war that there hardly remained a university at all. The colleges were utterly impoverished and almost devoid of students, the residence halls left in a universal state of disrepair by the soldiers and courtiers who had occupied them and the books of some libraries stolen: education was at a standstill.

This shocking condition was not to last long, however, and when Oxford fell to the parliamentary armies in 1648, the Puritans lost little time in purging the faculty of its Royalist sympathizers and instituting some badly needed reforms. Unfortunately, the zeal of the reformers outweighed their educational insight, and instead of instituting academic reforms, long overdue at even prerevolutionary Oxford, they concentrated exclusively on reforms of conduct. They closed the alehouses, increased church attendance, and tried to lure back the students and faculty by producing order where the war had left chaos. But even these unimaginative changes were enough to make Oxford once more into an educational institution, and if the Cromwellians did nothing to revise the out-of-date curriculum, H. R. Fox-Bourne points out that they at least had the virtue of recognizing their ignorance in educational matters.[2] They tried to restore to Oxford the best that they knew, the tradition of medieval Scholasticism that had existed there prior to the Civil War. To this end they employed the most competent non-Royalist scholars they could find to run the university. So it happened that the curriculum that Locke followed during his undergraduate years at Oxford was in form very much like that which he had followed during his five years at Westminster: Greek and Latin and some Hebrew, lectures in logic, metaphysics, and moral philosophy. Aristotle was still the Philosopher, in diluted medieval form, and the principal method of demonstrating academic achievement was the public disputation, attendance at which was required of all undergraduates.

From all the evidence available, it appears that Locke had a low opinion of his undergraduate education. He thought that the technique of formal disputation turned a man into "an insignificant wrangler, opinionated in discourse,'' and that the Aristotelian philosophy he was taught was "perplexed with obscure terms and useless questions,''[3] and anything but conducive to the increase in learning. He was impatient with the emasculated Aristotelianism that formed the staple of his intellectual diet, and it was only his study of geometry in his third year that brought forth any favorable words from him concerning his Oxford education.

In spite of his dissatisfaction with the state of learning at Oxford, however, he did well enough to be awarded his bachelor of arts in 1656 and his master of arts three years later. In the same year he was elected a senior student of Christ Church, and in 1660 he took the position of lecturer in Greek and tutor to approximately ten students at a time. Although he disapproved of the medieval Aristotelianism upon which he had to lecture, he did find Aristotle's metaphysics and natural philosophy more to his liking. He supplemented his regular reading with study of the *Politics* and *Nicomachean Ethics,* and later in life he expressed his belief that "No man can pass for a scholar that is ignorant of the Greek tongue...because amongst the Grecians is to be found the original, as it were the foundations of all that learning which we have in this part of the world."[4] This intimate knowledge of the writings of Aristotle and their medieval interpretations, along with his enthusiasm for the *Politics* and *Ethics,* was to have profound effects on his future philosophy and social thought. W. Von Leyden has noted the Aristotelian notions and direct quotations from the *Nicomachean Ethics* in Locke's early *Essays on the Law of Nature* and has concluded, "it was the original text, not the Aristotle of the Schoolmen, that interested him."[5] J. W. Gough has traced some of Locke's political ideas to Aristotelian distinctions (although via a long line of Roman and Scholastic writers),[6] and several people have mentioned casually the apparently direct influence of Aristotle on Locke's economic theories.[7] Even in his epistemology, it is likely that his extensive reading of Aristotle was a major influence on his work, although Locke claims his greatest debt was to Descartes and would have denied this Aristotelian influence emphatically.

In 1663, Locke was elected censor of moral philosophy for Christ Church. Part of the duties of this annually elected office was to deliver a series of lectures, and Locke chose the topic "The Law of Nature." Although he never published these lectures, he retained them in his possession and revised them extensively until about 1665, after which he never bothered with them again. In spite of this apparent neglect, Von Leyden contends that these natural law writings became a premise upon which Locke built many of his later theories and over a period of forty years "provided Locke with topics and inspiration which he turned to account in the building of his philosophy."[8] To a certain extent this also applies to the building of his economic theory.

At the time of Locke's election as censor of moral philosophy, he had a fundamental decision to make concerning his future at Oxford. Of the sixty senior studentships open at Christ Church, fifty-five were designated for the clergy, two were in law, two were in medicine, and one was in moral philosophy. For a time Locke contemplated taking holy orders to secure a permanent place at Oxford, but he could never quite bring himself to do so. Finally, in 1663, he decided to abandon any pretense of preparing to enter the clergy and instead decided to try for one of the studentships in medicine. It might seem arbitrary for a lecturer in Greek suddenly to decide to study medicine, but in fact the decision was based on an interest in the subject which Locke had been cultivating for several years.

In Locke's day, medicine was still being taught out of the works of Galen, Hippocrates, and Aristotle, and a student received a degree by being proficient in these ancient classics rather than as a result of any familiarity with practical healing methods. Bacon's experimental method was becoming more and more accepted, however, and was being applied to the study of medicine by men such as John Wilkins, brother-in-law of Oliver Cromwell, who came to Oxford with the parliamentary leader; Thomas Wallis, a practicing physician; Ralph Bathurst; and Thomas Goddard, warden of Merton College. These devoted empiricists, along with several others, including Sir William Petty who had by the time of Locke's arrival already left Oxford, formed a club devoted to the pursuit of experimental philosophy which met regularly in Wilkins's rooms to provide discussion of the members' work. This group later grew into the Royal Society and accepted John Locke as one of its earliest and most respected members.[9]

Locke was introduced to the work of these advocates of experimental science early in his Oxford career by his friend Richard Lower, a young medical student who had himself already made several discoveries about the feasibility of blood transfusions and the role of the heart in the circulation of the blood. It did not take long for the interests of the young John Locke to be sparked by this radical new experimental approach to learning. The dreary drills of Westminster and the artificial disputations which formed the basis of his education at Oxford seemed stale and unexciting by comparison. He became an enthusiastic advocate of empirical methods, and as early as 1652, his first year at Oxford, he began to keep a medical notebook in which he wrote down new remedies and bits of information on illness that came to his attention. He kept some kind of medical record for the rest of his life.

Locke began studying medicine in his spare time while still an undergraduate and continued almost full time after receiving his master's degree in 1658. His study was focused not on eventually entering into his own practice, but rather on the pursuit of medicine as experimental chemistry, the approach that was sanctioned by the experimental club. Locke's enthusiasm for experimentation caused him to be drawn to the laboratory in the High Street presided over by Robert Boyle, the leader of the Oxford empiricists. Boyle, originally part of a London group dedicated to pursuing experimental science called the Invisible College, had taken up residence in Oxford in 1654, but probably did not meet Locke until 1660. It was not until 1664 that the two men became closely involved with one another, when Locke began to follow the experiments Boyle and his group were making to study the problem of human respiration. But the friendship must have grown quickly, for the following year, while Locke was out of the country on a diplomatic mission to Brandenburg, the correspondence between the two men was the correspondence of two friends. The letters dealing mostly with chemical discoveries and metallurgic wonders reveal the closeness of their mutual interests, one of which was a common belief in alchemy, a belief with which Isaac Newton was to become increasingly impatient in later years.

Boyle, being older and more established than Locke, always dominated the relationship. It was Locke who aided Boyle with his experiments, and it was Locke who turned to Boyle for advice in scientific matters. Although Locke eventually became a good physician, Boyle was always the more creative scientist of the two, an evaluation with which Locke would have been the first to agree. Neither was Boyle's influence limited to the scientific realm, since it was as a result of his association with Boyle that Locke first became interested in philosophy. In the seventeenth century, under the term ''experimental philosophy,'' science and philosophy were undivided; both aimed at discovering the truths of nature through the use of empirical methods. To the seventeenth century empiricists, the *méthode* of Descartes was particularly appealing, as was the Greek atomism that was being revived by Pierre Gassendi. It was Boyle who first introduced Locke to the works of these two philosophers as well as to his own corpuscular theory of matter which became the starting point for Locke's famous *Essay Concerning Human Understanding*. But even in this realm, Locke always acknowledged his debt to Boyle. It was only in the opinions of his contemporaries and those of future generations that Locke was considered to have far surpassed Boyle as a philosopher.

Because of Locke's independent study of medicine from 1658 on, he tried to get permission to take his bachelor's and doctor's degree in medicine at the same time rather than go through the formal preparations for both, which would have entailed several more years' attendance at lectures and disputations. Although he got a recommendation from Clarendon, the vice-chancellor of the university, for the dispensation he desired, the medical faculty never approved it and finally Locke abandoned his attempt. Instead, he petitioned the king and was granted permission to retain his studentship without taking holy orders or applying himself to any particular field. Thus, even though he finally entered into private practice and made some reputation for himself as a physician, he never was awarded a doctorate in medicine from Oxford University. Yet it was in his capacity as a physician that he first met the man who was to shape the next twenty years of his life, Anthony Ashley Cooper (called "Ashley"), later the first earl of Shaftesbury.

In the summer of 1666, Ashley visited Oxford to drink some medical waters which John Locke secured for him at the request of David Thomas, a physician whom Locke was assisting at the time. Ashley and Locke seem to have developed an immediate rapport, and soon afterwards Locke was invited to join Ashley's household in London as resident physician. Locke accepted the invitation and thus stepped into a world totally removed from his scholarly life at Oxford.

Ashley was a politician in one of the most exciting political eras in England's history. His speciality was trade, and his chief interest was in stockholding and colonial expansion. He was alternately a Whig and a Tory, preferring to align himself with positions rather than parties. His major loyalty was to whatever would increase the trading advantage of the nation, and this included religious toleration, of which he was an enthusiastic supporter. Maurice Cranston's description of him is apt:

> Ashley opposed religious persecution because religious persecution divided a nation, drove many of its most industrious citizens to emigrate, and generally impeded commercial development. He saw more clearly than most Englishmen of his time how colonial expansion and international trade could be made to bring enormous fortunes to investors like himself and at the same time increase the wealth and power of the country as a whole. The example of Holland had taught him how trade and toleration could flourish splendidly together. He was the complete progressive capitalist in politics; he might almost have been invented by Marx.[10]

Some of Ashley's ideas and attitudes could not help but rub off on the restless Oxford don whom he took to live in his household.

The first few years of Locke's association with Ashley were spent primarily in the practice of medicine, but medicine was not Locke's only concern in Ashley's household. Although he did perform one of the first successful operations on a suppurating hydatid abscess of the liver on none other than Lord Ashley himself, it was for his other talents that Ashley gradually came to value him most. In fact, it was probably the excellent results of the operation that inspired his increasing confidence. According to Ashley's grandson, the third earl of Shaftesbury: "After this cure, Mr. Locke grew so much in esteem with my grandfather that as great a man as he had experienced him in physics, he looked upon this but as the least part. He encouraged him to turn his thoughts another way, nor would he suffer him to practise physic except in his own family and as a kindness to some particular friend."[11] As it turned out, this "other way" was far more important to the world than any of Locke's contributions in the field of medicine.

After Locke's successful treatment of Ashley's illness, he became much more a secretary and confidant than a physician, concerned in all the matters which concerned his friend. Among the most important at that time were problems of trade with which Ashley dealt in his capacity as member of the Privy Council Committee for Trade and the Plantations, and as chief member of the Lords Proprietor of Carolina, of which Locke became secretary in 1668. During that year there was much parliamentary agitation concerning a proposal to lower the official rate of interest to four per cent, a policy which had been advocated by Sir Josiah Child in two pamphlets published in 1668. It is likely that the contemporary discussion of the proposal, to which he was exposed through his association with Ashley, caused Locke to channel his thoughts toward an economic problem for the first time. The result was a paper (never published but forming the basis of his later writings on interest) entitled "Some of the Consequences that are like to follow upon Lessening of Interest to 4 Percent."[12] As William Letwin has said, the paper was "the work of an amateur"[13] who had had little contact with economic problems, yet in spite of its many flaws it displayed its author's "native talent for economics."[14] Among the contributions noted by Letwin in this early paper on trade were an objective evaluation of the gainers and losers by a lowering of the interest rate, a clear statement of the velocity of money, and the use of the concepts of real income and a natural rate of interest. These few insights were of minor importance, however, compared with the greater importance of the paper in stimulating Locke to think about economics in an abstract manner for the first time.

Much of his speculation on economics, exhibited both in that early paper and in his subsequent work over the next thirty years or so, was undoubtedly based on the practical experience he obtained as Ashley's companion in both the economic and political arena during the years of their association. In 1672, Ashley rose to the peak of his career, becoming lord high chancellor of England and the first earl of Shaftesbury. The following year, he lost his exalted position but not his new title, and still remained in the thick of the political struggle of Parliament versus King Charles. Locke appears to have aided the now earl of Shaftesbury and held minor offices during this time. In 1672, at Shaftesbury's urging, the Council of Trade and Plantations was formed with Shaftesbury as president. A year later Locke became secretary. The council lasted for only two years, but during this time it was Locke's duty as secretary to search out and present facts about conditions in and legislation proposed by the colonies as well as problems of foreign and domestic trade including those of charter companies. Locke himself became a member of a charter company organized by Shaftesbury in 1672, and this, along with his duties on the council, probably did much to mature his knowledge of trade and money.

Shaftesbury's fortunes began to wane in 1674, and the council was dissolved at the same time that he was dismissed from all offices for plotting against the king. Since Locke's position depended on Shaftesbury's, for a time Locke too seemed to retire from public life. He returned to Oxford where, in 1675, he was awarded his bachelor of medicine degree and one of the two medical studentships at Christ Church, and given permission to practice medicine. His recent taste of the larger world, however, probably made it difficult for him to return to the quiet life of an Oxford don, for instead of once again settling down to teach he left Oxford to go to France, where he remained for the next three years observing the mores of the country and noting down what he observed in his journal.[15]

In the following years, Shaftesbury's fortunes were erratic. In 1676 he was sent to the Tower for a year, but within a year of his release he succeeded in toppling his strongest rival, pushing a habeas corpus bill through parliament, and thwarting an alliance between King Charles and the king of France that would have established a Catholic monarch on the British throne. Shaftesbury finally pushed his luck too far, however, unsuccessfully trying to get Charles's bastard son, the Protestant duke of Monmouth, named legitimate heir to the throne instead of the duke of York, Charles's Catholic brother. This time when Charles dismissed him from his offices, Shaftesbury would not be able to rebound again.

For the next four years (1679–83), Shaftesbury was deeply involved in the abortive Monmouth Rebellion, while Locke was quietly living at Oxford and being very careful not to say or do anything that could be construed as being the least bit seditious. His care was occasioned by the fact that all associates of Shaftesbury were under constant surveillance, and Locke had been somewhat more than an associate. Evidently his caution paid off because nothing could ever be proved linking him to either Shaftesbury or the plot during these years, even though there is excellent circumstantial evidence that Locke was not so aloof from the plotting as he wished to appear. This evidence is his *Two Treatises of Government,* a political essay attacking the divine right of kings argument espoused by Sir Robert Filmer and justifying a change of rulers when the existing ruler no longer protects the interests of his subjects, which according to a likely hypothesis was composed in 1681, during the height of the revolutionary planning.[16] In other words, Locke at this time, while outwardly leading a quiet scholarly life, was most probably composing a work that would provide a philosophical basis for the revolution that his mentor was busily planning. But before Locke's revolutionary tract could be published (if indeed he planned to publish it at all), Shaftesbury was found out and was forced into hiding in Holland where he died in 1683, an exile from the country whose destiny he had worked so hard to shape. The king at once began a purge of Shaftesbury sympathizers, and Locke himself felt threatened enough to go to Holland at once, to reside for a while under an assumed name, until England was once again a safe place for a Whig.

Locke's six years in Holland were spent in furious intellectual activity. He availed himself of every opportunity to meet with scholars and theologians, and when he was not engaging in learned discourse he was engaged by his philosophical works. These years were devoted to completing his *Essay Concerning Human Understanding,* which he had begun in 1671 while in Shaftesbury's household. In addition, he wrote a draft of his *Thoughts Concerning Education* and nearly all the reviews published in the *Bibliothèque universelle* between July 1687 and February 1688. In 1688 William of Orange successfully deposed the Catholic James II from the British throne, and in 1689 Locke crossed the channel to England on the same ship that carried Queen Mary.

During his first year back in England, Locke quickly published the results of his years of work, *An Essay Concerning Human Understanding,* the *Letter Concerning Toleration* (containing ideas he was first convinced of by Shaftesbury), and the *Two Treatises of Government,* only the first of which bore his name. Its success as well as his "meritorious exile" succeeded in turning him into what Letwin has called "a sort of minor prophet,"[17] and he began to be recommended for important posts and sought after for advice on various public problems. He had his choice of positions but, for reasons of health, at first accepted only a minor appointment as commissioner of appeals. What followed, however, was not the studious semiretirement one would expect of a physically infirm philosopher, but instead the most active and politically influential period of Locke's life. He published no less than five major works and several minor papers on five different subjects during this decade, and established several political clubs as a means of making his views on policy measures known. He was able to influence Parliament to defeat the Act for the Regulation of Printing and was partly

13

responsible for designing the currency reform and recoinage undertaken by Parliament in 1696. The pinnacle of his public career came in 1695–96, when he was instrumental in reorganizing the old Committee for Trade as the Board of Trade, with himself as the dominant commissioner. He remained an active, though sickly, member until 1700, when his failing health along with the ascendancy of his political rivals caused him to retire to Oates, the home of an old and dear friend, Lady Masham, until his death in 1704.

## ECONOMIC WRITINGS

For the purpose of an intellectual biography, the years of Locke's life from 1690 to 1700 are probably the least important of any. He did his original thinking from 1650 to 1690, and his important writing during the last ten of those forty years. Indeed, we need concern ourselves at all only with the years 1680–90, because Locke's political concerns during this time caused him to revise and put into final form his thoughts on economic problems.

In 1681, a bill was once again before Parliament to lower the official rate of interest to four per cent, and again it was supported by Sir Josiah Child, who published a revised version of his 1668 paper concerning interest rates. By the time the bill was introduced in November 1691, Locke had already been revising his earlier papers on interest for over a year. He finished his revision, now entitled *Some Considerations of the Consequences of the Lowering of Interest and Raising the Value of Money*,[18] in time to have some influence on the outcome of the vote, but his influence was insufficient to sway Parliament to his side. In January 1692, the House of Commons passed a modified bill to lower the rate of interest to five per cent in spite of Locke's well-reasoned opinions. There is evidence that Locke's arguments were heard during the Parliamentary debate, but Locke's friend Edward Clarke wrote: ''I am satisfied that if an angel from Heaven had managed the debate, the votes would have been the same as now. For it is not reason, but a supposed benefit to the borrower that has passed the bill.''[19]

Although this was a defeat for Locke's arguments concerning interest rates, there was still another problem that Locke considered even more important to the welfare of the nation: the deteriorating state of British coin. Hammered coin was easily clipped and therefore unacceptable outside of England, while full-weight, milled money was undervalued domestically and therefore either melted down at home or exported abroad. Locke viewed this as being inimical to healthy trade and a subtle form of theft. He urged reform of the coinage in *Some Considerations,* where he advocated allowing clipped money to circulate at its real value rather than at its face value until it could be called in and recoined at the old standard. This section of *Some Considerations* had no effect on the Parliament of 1692, but Locke had another chance to try to convince them of his argument a few years later.

In 1695 the rapidly deteriorating state of England's currency convinced Parliament that something had to be done about recoinage, and the government called upon William Lowndes, the secretary of the treasury, for advice on the appropriate policy to follow. Lowndes suggested a general currency depreciation of twenty-five per cent and a rating of coin above its value as silver, both diametrically opposed to Locke's earlier proposals. Locke, known to have an interest in recoinage, was asked to comment on the suggestion, and the result was a second major pamphlet, again published anonymously, entitled *Further Considerations Concerning Raising the Value of Money,*[20] which once again argued for recoinage at full value. This time Locke was more successful in his partisanship, and the basic outline of his scheme was adopted.[21]

These two essays published five years apart, along with *Short Observations on a Printed Page,* a minor pamphlet that added little to Locke's economic analysis, and a few scattered

15

papers, comprise Locke's total published output on economic problems.[22] Both major essays were intended as polemical tracts to influence government policy, and both were well received and widely read at their time of publication. Although only the second fulfilled Locke's purpose for writing in that the policy proposed was actually adopted, it is mostly a rehash in stronger language of the coinage section in the first and far inferior in intellectual value. *Some Considerations* is an abstract piece of writing that makes significant contributions to economic science. It was the direct result of twenty years of conscious attention to problems of trade and money and the indirect result of even more years of study of related fields. Locke's economic theories show the influence of Aristotle, the medieval Scholastics, and the natural law theorists he read in his youth, of the empirical sciences he admired so much in his early manhood, and of the realities of the economic world he was made aware of by Shaftesbury. What these economic theories were that had been influenced by such an exalted array of sources is the subject to which we shall now turn our attention.

# TWO

# Theory of Value

THE PLACE to begin a discussion of John Locke's economic theories is with his theory of value. It is true of any economist that his economic policy ultimately reflects the kind of value theory to which he subscribes, but this is especially true of Locke. While value theory is by no means the main emphasis of Locke's economic writings, nevertheless it forms the basis of his whole economic analysis and economic policy. It was his one tool, his one model for dealing with all economic problems. His value theory provided him with not only an explanation of the prices of commodities, but in addition a theory of money, of interest, of rents, and of foreign exchange. If there is any one remarkable aspect of Locke's economics, it is the consistency with which he applied his theory of value to economic problems and the degree to which his analysis yielded satisfactory explanations.[1]

It is perhaps astonishing, then, that very little of what Locke says on the subject of value and price is new in itself. Antecedents can be found for most of his ideas in the writings of seventeenth-century mercantilists and both early and late Scholastics, and often what seems new in Locke had already been at least implied by Sir William Petty several decades earlier. In fact, the whole tenor of *Some Considerations* is that of a reasonable, well-informed man who is stating what everyone already knows and who is amazed by the reluctance of legislators and businessmen to recognize the obvious. So completely does he take for granted that he is merely setting down in consistent form what is common knowledge that he gives no indication of which of his ideas are new and which are borrowed.[2] But it is believed that Locke did very little reading of contemporary economic tracts before he wrote *Some Considerations,* however.[3] Much of the resemblance of Locke's theories to others of his day therefore is probably the result of secondhand discussions of economic questions, and most of it is merely apparent, frequently consisting in similar vocabulary only. The real influences on Locke's economic thought were more remote, coming primarily from a combination of his reading of Aristotle, the Scholastics, and his contemporaries Grotius and Pufendorf on the one hand, and his own personal observation of economic problems on the other. While he had occasional flashes of originality in his theoretical work, his real contribution to the development of value theory is the manner in which he was able to fuse the many existing pieces of analysis into a comprehensive theory of economic behavior. He restates the commonplace in such a way as to formulate a systematic economic theory with the determination and functioning of price as its cornerstone.

## VALUE OF GOODS

A useful place to begin a discussion of Locke's theory of value is with his treatment of the customary distinction between intrinsic value and market value. This distinction, of course, was first made by Aristotle, who identified both a value in use and a value in exchange for any good.[4] It was common throughout the Middle Ages and into the seventeenth century to make such a distinction when discussing the value of goods, generally with the purpose of trying to explain why some goods which have a great "intrinsic" value (i.e., are very useful in supporting human life) often have a very low exchange value, and vice versa, as in the familiar diamonds–water paradox.[5] Frequently the statement of the difference between use value and exchange value was a means to explain the role of scarcity in the determination of market price. Locke uses the distinction, however, to introduce to the reader the factors which he believes determine the relative value of goods. He defines relative value as follows:

1. That the intrinsick natural worth of any thing, consists in its fitness to supply the necessities or serve the conveniencies of human life; and the more necessary it is to our being, or the more it contributes to our well-being the greater is its worth: but yet,
2. That there is no such intrinsick natural settled value in anything, as to make any assigned quantity of it, constantly worth any assigned quantity of another.
3. The marketable value of any assigned quantities of two or more commodities are pro hic et nunc, equal when they will exchange one for another.[6]

In other words, while Locke may agree that things are valuable in some absolute sense in relation to how well they satisfy the needs and desires of human beings (an argument he also makes in the *Second Treatise*),[7] price or market value refers only to the quantities of goods that can be exchanged for each other or their value relative to one another, and there is no such thing as a fixed or absolute relative value. Instead, relative values depend strictly upon "some proportion which that commodity bears to something else." This proportion he identifies as "the proportion of their quantity to the vent."[8] Locke then goes on to explain what determines the quantity and the vent of a good and how changes in the quantity and vent lead to changes in market prices.

Locke's account of the determination of prices has often been characterized as an early version of supply-and-demand analysis where *quantity* was his term for *supply* and *vent* his term for *demand*.[9] If this is an accurate description of Locke's value theory, his supply-and-demand analysis was of a most primitive kind. Although some statements of his about the effects of low rates of interest on the supply of loanable funds indicate that he understood there to be a positive relationship between price and quantity supplied, and with a bit of charitable interpretation we can find passages that indicate an inverse relationship between price and quantity demanded, the whole thrust of Locke's discussion on price is in terms of the effects on prices of changes in quantity and changes in vent. In neoclassical terminology, he seems to be talking about shifts in the supply-and-demand functions rather than movements along the functions. Even more disturbing is the fact that Locke's ''supply-and-demand'' analysis was not even the most advanced for his time. While most mercantilists of the era previous to Locke had understood how quantity (or scarcity) affected the value of goods, a notion that can be traced back at least as far as the Scholastics of the late fifteenth century,[10] Locke's own contemporaries Nicholas Barbon[11] and Dudley North[12] were both formulating relatively sophisticated supply-and-demand theories of price determination. In fact, John Law writing in 1704 considered Locke's account of price determination to be a step backward because he used the term *vent* instead of *demand,* which Law considered an analytically more useful term. Law's criticism was that whereas demand could be different from the number of sales in any given time period, vent was a term which meant disposing of goods by sale and must be identical to the number of transactions made.[13] While Law acknowledged that Locke probably meant *demand,* the fact that Locke used the term *vent* at all suggested a relatively old-fashioned understanding of the determination of market price, even for 1690. It might be argued that since Locke wrote most of *Some Considerations* twenty years before it was published, the use of *vent* might reflect nothing more than a failure to bring his terminology up to date. On the other hand, it might instead be that the term *vent* was particularly appropriate for the kind of price theory Locke was developing. Before we explore that possibility, however, it will be useful to note the similarities between Locke's formulations and later supply-and-demand theory and his contributions to that theory.

Locke explained that price depends upon the proportion of the quantity of a good to its vent, where price increases are associated with increases in vent and price decreases associated with increases in quantity.[14] As we have already indicated, in neoclassical terms his analysis for the most part is concerned with explaining price changes resulting from shifts in the demand or supply curves, with very little analysis of the determinants or characteristics of supply curves or demand curves themselves. Generally, he regards supply or quantity as given, although his discussion of the relationship between the rate of interest and the supply of loanable funds is a notable exception. Here Locke indicates that if the rate of interest is held below the market rate, the quantity of loanable funds will fall, as lenders hold back their money at "such a disproportion of profit, to risk," while increases in the rate of interest are seen to induce increased foreign lending in England.[15] Clearly, in this instance Locke is describing a direct relationship between price and quantity supplied, although he did not generalize this relationship to other goods. One wonders if the reason for his failure to describe a positive price–quantity relationship for the supply of other goods was that he did not believe such a relationship existed or simply that interest was the major topic of his essay and he saw no need to compare the supply of loanable funds to the supply of other goods.

While Locke's treatment of quantity, or supply, is scanty, his treatment of the vent of goods, or demand, is very rich in similarities to modern analysis. In fact he describes changes in vent occurring because of changes in price, changes in tastes, and changes in the price of substitute goods. He also implies, as did Petty before him, the concept of elasticity of demand.

21

As Locke saw it, vent changed primarily as a result of the number of people wishing to purchase a product or, as he put it, "The price of any commodity rises or falls, by the proportion of the number of buyers and sellers."[16] If a great number of people decide to buy one product instead of another, the price of the first increases while the price of the second decreases, and vice versa; the quantity of both commodities is assumed constant. In addition, the proportion of the total money income people designate for the purchase of a commodity is also important in determining price, or as he puts it, "The vent of any commodity comes to be increased or decreased as a greater part of the running cash of the nation is designed to be laid out by several people at the same time rather in that, than another."[17] This reference to the proportion of the "running cash of the nation" will take an even greater significance when we examine the relationship between the value of goods and the value of money.

Locke explains that while price depends exclusively upon the proportion between quantity and vent, the vent of any thing "depends upon its necessity or usefulness, as convenience, or opinion guided by fancy or fashion shall determine."[18] In other words, the vent of a commodity depends upon the subjective evaluation of individuals as to the necessity or usefulness of a good. If several people all at once decide that one good is more desirable than they previously realized, the vent will increase and so will the price. Once again he emphasizes that "intrinsic value" alone will have no influence on the exchange value of a good unless it also changes the quantity and vent of the good.[19]

He goes on to categorize goods according to the responsiveness of vent, or quantity demanded, to changes in price. The first category of goods he discusses is "the necessaries, or conveniencies of life, and the consumable commodities subservient there unto." The necessaries are peculiar in that "men will give any portion of money for whatsoever is absolutely necessary rather than go without it. And in such things the scarcity of them alone makes their prices.''[20] In neoclassical terminology, Locke seems to be saying that insofar as a good is absolutely necessary to existence, its market demand will be totally inelastic and supply will determine the price.[21] Food is an example of such a good in Locke's estimation, where even quality has little influence on price determination since the amount that is needed to sustain life will be demanded regardless of price or excellence of the product, until the total expenditure on food equals one's entire income.

Unlike with necessities, however, the quantity demanded of conveniences will vary as price changes because ''things absolutely necessary for life must be had at any rate; but things convenient will be had only as they stand in preference with other conveniences: and therefore in any one of these commodities, the value rises only as its quantity is less, and vent greater, which depends upon its being preferred to other things, in its consumption.''[22] Conveniences have more elastic demand schedules than necessities because there are substitutes available, so if the price of one good rises, the consumers can switch to purchasing a cheaper good which satisfies the same use. The rate at which people are willing to substitute one good for another depends upon the relative preferences they have for one good over the other. Locke's example here is between wheat and oats, both foods which can satisfy hunger. If there is a shortage of all food, supply alone determines price, but if the shortage is in wheat alone, men will be unwilling to give any amount of money rather than do without it, and will instead shift some of their food expenditure from the (in general) preferred wheat to the less pleasant-tasting (in Locke's opinion) and therefore less preferred oats. He maintained that

> men no question would give far more for wheat than
> oats, as being the healthier, pleasanter, and more
> convenient food: but since oats would serve to supply
> that absolute necessity of sustaining life, men would
> not rob themselves of all other conveniences of life,

by paying all their money for wheat when oats, that
are cheaper, though with some inconvenience, would
supply that defect.[23]

This passage implicitly is describing substitution among
goods at the margin.

The demand for the last category of goods that Locke
chooses to discuss, luxuries, is really an exception to the
general demand relationship which holds for most goods.
Locke's condemnation of luxury spending speaks eloquently
of the influence of his early Puritan background on his later
thinking. Luxuries are defined as rare and foreign commodities that are not necessary for a comfortable life and which
constitute not only a waste of personal resources, but also a
drain on the gold supply of a country. The desire for them is
not even rational, let alone admirable, "for it being vanity,
not use, that makes the expensive fashion of your people, the
emulation is, who shall have the finest, that is, the dearest
things, not the most convenient or useful."[24] Given the
eccentricities of the luxury-seekers, however, it is futile to
attempt to control their consumption. They obey laws which
are exactly the contrary of the normal demand relationship,
and official discouragement makes them only more desirable:

> Fashion is, for the most part, nothing but the
> ostentation of riches, and therefore the high price of
> what serves to that, rather increases than lessens its
> vent. The contest and glory is in the expense, not the
> usefulness of it; and people are then thought and
> said to live well when they can make a show of rare
> and foreign things, and such as their neighbors can-
> not go the price of.[25]

Fortunately for the economy, such extravagant and frivolous
people make up only a small percentage of the buying public, and their behavior pertains only to a select group of
goods. For all other goods, price and quantity vented are
inversely related.

There are several interesting principles illustrated in Locke's analysis of the determination of price of most goods. Locke obviously realized that goods are not demanded in a vacuum, but only as they stand in relation to other goods in the economy. The quantity vented of any good at a given price depends on the necessity of that good to the sustaining of life, the preferences people have for that good, and the price of substitutes for the good.[26] He made no specific reference to the income variable in the demand relationship, perhaps because he considered income a parameter of longer duration than the others in his model. People decide how much of a usually constant budget to allocate to expenditures upon various goods depending upon the magnitudes of the other determining variables. Although his classification of various kinds of goods implies the concept of elasticity, his development of it is understandably deficient. He never specifically mentions the effects on total revenue that price changes have on goods with different kinds of elasticities— the defining characteristic of a concept of elasticity of demand—but he does mention the possibility that a rise in farm product prices will cause the consumer "to make as sparing use of them as he can that he may save his money for other necessities or creditable expenses,"[27] implying that total expenditure will fall and hurt the farmer. His comparison of the price determination of necessities and near necessities indicates that he had at least some idea of the consequences of different elasticities of demand on changes in price.

## PROPORTIONALITY THEORY OF PRICE

In light of the foregoing analysis, one is perhaps led to ask: If Locke's price theory was not an early version of supply-and-demand analysis (as we hinted above), then what was it? We can begin to answer that question first by examining exactly what Locke meant by the term *vent*. *Vent* is a term which means rate of sales to final consumers per time period:

The vent is nothing else, but the passing of commodities from one owner to another in exchange; and is then called quicker, when a greater quantity of any species of commodity, is taken off from the owners of it, in an equal space of time.

This vent is regulated, i.e. made quicker or slower, as greater or less quantities of any saleable commodity are removed out of the way, and course of trade; separated from publick commerce; and no longer lie within the reach of exchange.[28]

He goes on to explain how vent can be increased, emphasizing the fact that vent refers only to final sales to consumers:

1. By consumption, when the commodity in its use is destroyed, as meat, drink, and clothes, etc. all that is so consumed is quite gone out of the trade of the world. 2. By exportation; and all that is so carried away, is gone out of the trade of England, and concerns Englishmen no more in the price of their commodities among themselves for their own use, than if it were out of the world. 3. By buying and laying up for a man's private use. . . . All these three terminating at last in consumption of all commodities, (excepting only jewels and plate, and some few others which wear out but insensibly) may properly enough pass under that name.[29]

That is, vent increases if consumption (in any of its three forms—personal use, exportation, or hoarding) increases. In each case, the way to increase vent is to prevent resale of the article, an end clearly desired by sellers.[30] Obviously, Locke treated vent as a flow, a physical volume of sales per unit of time. Vent is not identical to the modern concept of demand, but seems to be closest in modern terminology to a point on a demand curve. The next question to ask, then, is how did Locke use this flow concept in his theory of price? What kind of model did he have for which a term such as *vent* was needed?

Unlike a modern price theorist, Locke did not see price as the result of the interaction of two functional relationships which are defined for a given moment in time. Instead, he always describes price as an exchange ratio which is determined by a set of proportions involving the quantity of a good (the stock available) and its vent (a flow). Most of the time, he claims that price is determined by the proportion between the quantity of one good and its vent compared with that between the quantity and vent of the good for which it is exchanged.[31] In addition, he occasionally also compares this proportion with the proportion of money income devoted to purchasing the good in question.[32] Price will alter either through a change in the quantity and vent of one good or through a change in either the quantity or vent of the good for which it is exchanged. Specifically, price will increase if vent of a good increases "proportionably" to quantity and it will fall if vent falls "proportionably" to quantity. While it was common in mercantilist literature to identify high prices with scarcity and low prices with abundance, this particular formulation of price was unusual. The question that arises is whether Locke had any specific reason for stating his explanation of price determination in this way. Did Locke have any reason for explaining price as a proportion between the quantity and the vent of a set of goods? There are two possible explanations for Locke's way of stating economic laws: one reaches back into the distant past while the other appeals to more contemporary sources.

It should be pointed out that Locke was by no means the first to express economic relationships in terms of proportions. The practice begins at least with Aristotle, whose theory of exchange is based on mathematical proportions borrowed from the Pythagoreans. In his philosophy, Aristotle used mathematical proportions to explicate the problem of justice, in particular, the problem of justice in exchange. He sought some just means for equating the values exchanged by two parties based on the utility each derived from the goods given and received. According to one modern interpreter of Aristotle, the model he used was geometric mean to represent an exchange of equivalent values, where the component parts of the exchange involved both the goods to be exchanged and the two people engaging in the exchange.[33] Much of the medieval literature on exchange and the just price was based on Aristotle, and the idea of proportionality as the basis for exchange reappeared in this literature.[34] Locke, of course, was familiar with both Aristotle and the medieval Scholastics and may have assimilated into his own thought the idea that proportions were somehow the proper means for expressing relationships among economic variables, although he did not share the Aristotelian-Scholastic preoccupation with exploring the requirements for justice in exchange, at least not directly.

While Aristotle and the tradition he spawned might account for Locke's receptivity to using proportions in developing his theory of value, there is an even more convincing source for his formulations in his own century: contemporary natural science. It is very possible that Locke was using the terminology of contemporary science to explain the laws of economics as he understood them. The similarity is obvious when one considers the nature of many of the scientific discoveries of the seventeenth century: frequently they were framed in terms of mathematical proportions. Kepler had shown that the square of the period of the orbit of a planet is proportional to the cube of the mean distance from the sun; Leonardo that motive power is proportional to the weight of the body moved and the velocity impressed on it; Boyle that pressure and volume of gas are inversely proportional; and, finally, Newton, the culmination of the age, was postulating that the motion of the entire universe could be explained in terms of a single proportional law involving the distance and relative mass of heavenly bodies.[35] With the nature of these laws in mind, we must conclude that Locke's constant use of proportions between economic magnitudes in his economic works was at the very least an unconscious mimicking of the vocabulary of the natural sciences, and that he may even have been consciously attempting to use the newly discovered methods of the physical sciences to describe an exact causal relationship between changes in price and changes in the variables which determine it.[36]

Although Locke's proportionality theory of price may seem limited from the perspective of modern economic theory, Locke nevertheless managed to use it to good advantage. With it he was able to define economic goods, explain changes in relative prices, describe a circular flow of money and goods in the economy, and develop a quantity theory of money which was advanced for his age.

We see his proportionality theory of price first in his version of the famous diamonds–water paradox (but in this case, without the diamonds).

> What more useful and necessary things are there to the being or well-being of men, than air and water? And yet these generally have no price at all, nor yield any money: because their quantity is immensely greater than their vent, in most places of the world. But as soon as ever water (for air still offers itself everywhere, without restraint or inclosure, and therefore is no where of any price) comes anywhere to be reduced into any proportion to its consumption, it begins presently to have a price, and is sometimes sold dearer than wine.[37]

A good must have a quantity in *some finite proportion* to its vent (the ratio of quantity to vent must be less then infinity) for it to command a price. The actual price is determined specifically by the proportion which the quantity bears to the vent of the product. Price is directly proportional to the vent and inversely proportional to the quantity. Hence, when quantity is vastly greater than vent price will be zero. The price of a commodity increases or decreases "as it makes its

29

quantity or vent, greater or less, in proportion one to another,"[38] so if both quantity and vent change in the same proportion and in the same direction, price will remain the same.

But goods do not exist in isolation and the very concept of price implies that there are at least two goods involved in an exchange. Price must then be a proportion not only of quantity and vent of one good alone, but somehow reflect the proportions of quantity to vent of all the goods offered in exchange. Locke's second use of the term *proportionality* predictably tackled the problem of relative price.

The simplest form of exchange is barter, in which one good is exchanged directly for another. In such an exchange, the market value of one good is nothing other then the quantity of another good for which it will exchange. If one good suddenly becomes more scarce than it was before, less of it will be given for the same quantity of the other goods, in other words its price relative to the other goods increases. Relative prices are really, then, a series of exchange ratios of all the goods in the economy: "The marketable value of any assigned quantities of two or more commodities, are pro hic et nunc equal, when they will exchange one for another. As supposing one bushel of wheat, two bushels of barley, thirty pounds of lead, and one ounce of silver, will now in the market be taken for one another, they are then of equal worth."[39]

Barter prices are ambiguous, however, in that they do not clearly show an alteration in one good at a time. That one would have to give more of any other good in order to obtain the same amount of one particular good is the usual meaning of a price increase, but in expressing barter prices there is no guarantee that an alteration in the proportion of quantity to vent of another good does not take place at the same time. For an accurate expression of price, an entire set of ratios would have to be quoted for every good in the economy. To obviate this troublesome necessity, all prices are instead quoted in terms of one arbitrarily chosen commodity: a numeraire for the system. Any change in the proportion of the quantity to the vent of one particular commodity then will result in a change in the proportion of the commodity exchanging for a unit of the numeraire. In Locke's system of price determination, this is the major function of money, to make relative prices more conveniently expressed and "to reckon what the proportion of scarcity and vent of one commodity is to another."[40]

In Locke's view of the operation of the price system, then, the existence of a finite proportion between the quantity and the vent of a particular commodity assures that it has a market price, that it is an economic good; and the ratio of exchange between goods, their relative prices, is a function of the proportion of quantity to vent of each product. Money is no other than a commodity whose price is defined as unity. Because the money commodity bears this definitional distinction of being the "counter-balance to all other things purchaseable by it, and lying, as it were, in the opposite scale of commerce,"[41] the proportion of its quantity to its vent has a special importance to the determination of prices. In order to understand more fully the importance of this proportion, we must first look more closely at Locke's theory of money.

### THEORY OF MONEY

It can be argued that Locke developed his theory of value in *Some Considerations* solely to be able to explain the determinants of the value of money. The purpose of his writing on economics in the first place was after all to clear up what he saw to be current confusions about the interest rate and the price level, and he found the best way to do this was to present a general theory of value which provided a basis for a theory not only of money as a medium of exchange, but also of interest, rents, and capital values. We cannot overemphasize that it is this consistency in his approach that makes Locke's economics interesting and marks one of his major contributions to economic science. One important result of Locke's approach to economics was that by applying his value theory to the money commodity he was able to develop a quantity theory of money which had a theoretical basis in a general theory of value, rather than being simply a statement of an empirical observation, as so many previous "quantity theories" had been.

Locke's discussion of money can be divided into three parts: the origin of money; the requirements and functions of a money commodity; and the determinants of the value of money. The first two are important for establishing his philosophy of and attitude toward money in order to classify his monetary theory properly, while the third encompasses the portion of Locke's economics that has come to be best known, his quantity theory of money.

*Origin of money.* Locke's first discussion of money occurs not in his two economic works, but rather in the *Second Treatise of Government* where, in the context of his discussion of the societal organization within the state of nature, he describes the process by which money first came into common use.[42] The law of nature, the guiding force in the state of nature, required that no man waste any of the natural resources given in common to all mankind, and anything which a man allowed to decay or spoil while in his possession was considered to be equivalent to theft: "As much as anyone can make use of to any advantage of life before it spoils; so much he may by his labour fix a Property in. Whatever is beyond this, is more than his share, and belongs to others. Nothing was made by God for Man to spoil or destroy."[43] If a man subject to this prohibition were to produce more than he could consume or enjoy at once, he then had an incentive to find a means of preserving his surplus for future use. The most reasonable means of storing the excess would be to exchange his perishables for more durable commodities which would be preserved for long periods of time without deterioration. Any durable commodity would suffice, but if it were one which might depreciate significantly in value over long periods of time, it would be less effective as a store of value. Gold and silver were especially suitable, since not only were they durable, being virtually indestructible, but they were also slow to change their value. As they became an established store of value, men began accepting them in exchange for other commodities and, hence, their function as a medium of exchange was established. The two functions reinforced each other as these metals' suitability as a store of value made them acceptable to people in exchange, and their ready acceptance in exchange for commodities made them more reliable as stores of value. Thus, Locke maintained, men took otherwise worthless substances and agreed to put an imaginary value upon them for the sake of their own convenience.

The interesting feature of this account of the origin of money is that it fits so well into Locke's contract theory of the origins of civil society. This will be examined in greater detail in chapter 4, but for now it is enough to note that money came about through an implicit contract which enabled men to circumvent difficulties inherent in the state of nature. The choice of a specific commodity was arbitrary and based only on its suitability to its task. In fact, the ones chosen, gold and silver, had no value whatsoever to human life (no intrinsic value) to begin with and so derived a value only from universal agreement.[44]

*Requirements and functions of a money commodity.* In Locke's economic works, he takes the origin of money for granted and continues from there to enumerate the requirements for and the functions of money. The money commodity must be durable, divisible, universally acceptable, and scarce in order for it to function properly. These requirements were not new to economics; observed by Aristotle in the *Politics*,[45] they were well known to scholars from the time of the rediscovery of Aristotle's works in the Western world in the thirteenth century. But their enumeration was enlarged upon by Locke to make clear the various functions of money. Since money acts as both a store of value and a medium of exchange, it must not alter its value greatly or quickly; hence the need for it to be durable and scarce. Since money also functions as a unit of account, serving "both for counters and for pledges, and so carrying with it even reckoning, and security, that he that receives it shall have the same value for it again, of other things that he wants, whenever he pleases,"[46] it must also be easily divisible. As he implied in the *Second Treatise,* any commodity would have done as long as it fulfilled the requirements, but most substances have serious drawbacks. Locke gives several alternative examples: lead is easily divisible and durable, but it is too abundant and too prone to rapid changes in price to be a money commodity, while jewels are scarce enough and durable enough, but their value does not depend upon their "quantity alone," since it does not increase in strict proportion to their size.[47] Gold and silver are in every way, then, the most suitable money commodities.

Since money is in itself worthless, one would expect Locke to find paper as acceptable a money commodity as precious metals, but this he denied for what were essentially political reasons. Although money is an agreed-upon convenience that arises spontaneously in nature, and the money commodity has a value only by virtue of common consent, nevertheless what men have consented to value as money are quantities of gold and silver.[48] Men do not agree to accept paper as a medium of exchange, and so paper money does not enjoy either widespread acceptance at home or any acceptance at all in foreign trade. It is therefore not suitable for use as money.[49] This is true of token money too, which Locke regarded as little better than fraud.[50] A testament to his attitude is the fact that a full third of *Some Considerations,* as well as all of *Further Considerations,* is devoted to the folly of trying to alter the standard of value by changing the silver content of public coins. Although the original choice of the money commodity was an arbitrary one, Locke contends that once it was decided upon, it became "the thing bargained for, as well as the measure of the bargain."[51] The ruling authority should then have no hand in trying to alter the content of public coins, on two counts: because it would be defrauding the public, and because it is unable to effect any change in the value of silver. On the first count, gold and silver are "common pledges, whereby men are assured, in exchange for them to receive equally valuable things to those they parted with for any quantity of these metals."[52] An alteration in the silver content of coins by the public authority would make it difficult to determine the real value of coins and so would hinder this "exchange of equivalents." On the second count, an attempt to change the standard of value by altering the silver content of coins is doomed to failure anyway, because men contract for silver and not for a denomination or a stamp, "for it is only the quantity of silver in it [coin] that is, and eternally will be, the measure of its value."[53] If the government tries to cut the silver content of coins by one-third, all that will happen is that each individual coin will be worth one-third less than before. In this sense, Locke can be classified as a metallist, since we see he most definitely held that the value of money was the same as the value of the money commodity. He was no ordinary metallist, however, in that the reasons for his conclusions do not depend on a belief in any objective value of the money commodity, but rather on his understanding of its function.[54]

*Quantity theory of money.* When Locke says that it is the quantity of silver alone that is the measure of value, all he means is that people value twice as much silver twice as much, or that the purchasing power of silver bears a one-to-one correspondence to its quantity. This value expressible in its quantity is what Locke calls the intrinsic value of silver. This is a strange use of *intrinsic* in Locke's system since he has already categorized the value of silver as imaginary, but it does reflect a quality of silver that makes it useful as money.

But quantity in this sense has nothing to do with a quantity theory of money. The part of Locke's theory of money that has to do with a genuine quantity theory of money is found in his theory of the determinants of the market value of money.

Locke's basic premise is that money is a commodity and therefore subject to the same laws of value to which commodities are subject.[55] Like most commodities, it has a double value, a value in use and a value in exchange. Unlike with other commodities, however, the value of money in use is its ability to bring in an income to its owner—to be lent out for "use"—while its value in exchange is its purchasing power. Since this "double" value has been the source of some controversy in the Locke literature, we will first consider Locke's theory of the value of money in exchange and defer a discussion of his theory of interest until chapter 3. Since the price of a commodity is determined by the proportion of its quantity to its vent, the value of money will be determined in much the same way. Because it is universally acceptable in exchange for other goods, however, money represents a special case of commodities. Its major difference from other commodities is that people never have enough of it, and they are always willing to accept money in exchange for anything else. The demand for money then is very different from the demand for other commodities:

> Hence it is that other commodities have sometimes a quicker, sometimes a slower vent: for nobody lays out his money in them, but according to the use he has of them, and that has bounds. But everybody being ready to receive money without bounds, and keep it by him because it answers all things: therefore the vent of money is always sufficient, or more than enough. This being so, its quantity alone is enough to regulate and determine its value, without considering any proportion between its quantity and vent, as in other commodities.[56]

This paragraph is difficult to interpret, yet it is crucial to understanding Locke's quantity theory of money. The problem is in discovering what Locke meant by the statement that the vent of money is "always sufficient or more than enough." Sufficient for what purpose? He may mean no more than that money is always acceptable as a medium of exchange, but then his contention that "quantity alone is enough to... determine its value" is unintelligible. In fact, it is more in keeping with Locke's other statements about the vent of money to understand him as meaning that the demand for money either is constant or changes very slowly.

In modern terminology then, Locke seems to be saying that the demand for money as a medium of exchange will be constant and not subject to the whims of fashion which cause the demand for other commodities to change (another way of putting this is that Locke assumed the velocity of circulation of money was constant), which means that the value of money will be determined solely by the quantity available. To put it in Locke's vocabulary: price changes result from nonproportional changes in quantity and vent, but in the case of money, vent is constant, so any change in quantity will cause the proportion to change and so the value of money. If we add to this the observation that the value of money is really the inverse of the price level of goods in the economy, we can see that as the quantity of money increases, the price level must increase; and as the quantity of money decreases, the price level must decrease.

The statement that the value of money is regulated by its quantity alone forms the crux of Locke's quantity theory of money. The quantity theory of money has a long and much belabored history—just how long depends for the most part on how loosely one wishes to define "quantity theory."[57] One finds the influx of gold from the New World identified as the cause of sixteenth-century inflation in the writings of the Spanish Scholastics of the School of Salamanca, especially those of Azpilcueta Navarro in 1556.[58] Later Jean Bodin

37

described a direct relationship between quantity of money and price level in his famous "Response aux paradox de M. de Malestroict" in 1568. There he identified the major cause of the decline in the value of money over the past century as the increase in the quantity of precious metals flowing into Europe from the New World, rather than the debasement of the coinage, which was the older, more popular idea in France and, indeed, in most of northern Europe. The quantity idea as an explanation of inflation was quickly diffused throughout Europe, and by the end of the sixteenth century it had appeared in the writings of, among others, Luis Molina in Spain, Davanzati in Italy, and John Hales in England. None of these men developed a genuine quantity theory of money, however, since their observations were usually no more than an application of supply-and-demand theory to the commodity money.[59] There was little recognition of the special characteristics of money that make the determination of its value different from that of the value of any other commodity. As a result, the effect of increased quantities of money shared equal ranking with debasement as an explanation of inflation and as the basis for policy recommendations. Even by the seventeenth century, when the observation that "plentie of money maketh generally things deare" was commonplace in the works of men such as Gerald Malynes, Thomas Mun, Rice Vaughan, Simon Clement, and John Pollexfen,[60] there was no theoretical analysis that recognized the special character of money as a medium of exchange. Although Locke's theory of the value of money also starts out as a commodity theory (i.e., the value of money is equal to the value of the money commodity), he differs from his predecessors by recognizing the special function of the money commodity. This leads him to state that the money commodity has no value in itself (which is, of course, an overstatement) and functions only as a medium of exchange. Concluding therefore that demand for the money commodity plays no part in determining the value of money, and assuming that demand for money as a medium of exchange is constant, he further concluded that quantity alone determines the value of money. Assuming then a constant output of all other commodities, a given change in the quantity of money will bring forth a proportional change in the price level.[61]

To illustrate his theory of money, Locke is careful to distinguish between changes in prices brought about by changes in the quantity of money and changes in relative prices only. (Indeed, the difference between relative and absolute price is a major theme running through Locke's essays.) For example, he explains that the price of wheat rose 1,000 per cent during the two hundred years following the time of Henry VII, not because of any change in the proportion of quantity to vent of wheat, but because "there being ten times as much silver now in the world (the discovery of the West Indies having made the plenty) as there was then, it is nine tenths less worth now than it was at that time."[62] Of course, his example is not meant to imply that the same proportionality would apply to all goods.[63] He used wheat for his example because he believed that it was a commodity which maintained a stable proportion of quantity to vent over time and so would accurately reflect changes in the value of money. It was Locke's "market basket" for comparing changes in the price level. He further emphasized the proportionality between changes in money and the price level by saying that if a country were to lose half of its money supply but maintain the same level of output, one of two things would happen: Either half its products would go unsold, or the same number of products would sell at half the price.[64]

Clearly, unlike the early "quantity theorists," Locke had a quantity theory of the determination of the value of money based solely on the function of money as a medium of exchange, rather than simply an empirical explanation of an existing inflation based on supply-and-demand analysis. This interpretation is further reinforced by Locke's insistence that in an isolated economy, any amount of money would be sufficient for the purposes of exchange, since the price level would adjust to the quantity of money.[65] All that is lacking so far to make Locke's analysis a statement of the quantity theory of money as it has come to be known today is a recognition of the fact that the money side of the quantity equation is a flow rather than a stock: that there is a rate of turnover or a velocity of circulation of money that also plays a part in determining the value of money. Locke did, in fact, understand this and to some extent incorporated it into his theory of money.

The recognition of the velocity of money was not completely new in Locke. Sir William Petty, one of the first economists to apply statistical techniques (although decidedly primitive ones at best) to the study of economic problems, arrived at a concept of the velocity of money in the course of his typically mercantilist inquiry into how much money was required to "drive the Trade" of the country.[66] He wished to arrive at a numerical estimate and attacked the problem by estimating the payments habits of the community. The result was a formulation of the income velocity concept. If income payments were normally made once a week, $\frac{1}{52}$ of the total value of the yearly income bill would be necessary to support a given level of trade, whereas if payments were usually made every three months, one-fourth of the income bill would be necessary. Although from there it is a short step to saying that increased frequency of payments will perform the same function as an increase in the money supply, and hence velocity is directly proportional to the price level, Petty failed to take this step. Although Petty, like his contemporaries, understood the effect of changing quantities of money on the price level, his theory of the natural value of money was a cost-of-production theory. The value of silver, he believed, was determined by the cost of labor needed to mine it, which was in turn measured by the food eaten by an average worker in an average day. Increases in the quantity of silver mined might increase the price level, but this was only because improved mining techniques reduced the cost of production. So while Petty had all the elements necessary to arrive at a quantity theory of money, he never put them together. That was left to Locke.

Like Petty, Locke also attempted to calculate what amount of money the kingdom needed to support a given level of trade at a given price level, as a preliminary to which he too tried to estimate the "quickness of circulation" of the money supply. What is often overlooked in assessments of Locke's monetary economics, however, is the fact that the concept of velocity of circulation was implicit from the first in his explanation of how the value of money is determined. In this respect, Locke's quantity theory is superior to Petty's.

We remember that the quantity of money alone determines its value because the vent of money is "always sufficient," which means that unlike other commodities, the vent of money rarely varies. Since in Locke's terminology vent means a rate of turnover, it is obvious that vent is his way of explaining the velocity of money. In fact, given Locke's definition, vent is a much more appropriate term to use with regard to money than it is with regard to goods. His perception must have been something like this: For any one good there is a rate of turnover from seller to buyer which depends upon (a) the level of final consumption, (b) the level of exportation, and (c) the level of hoarding. For most goods, the level of consumption is the primary determinant of its vent, but that is subject to the vagaries of "fancy and fashion." Money is also a commodity in that it is offered in exchange for other goods, but it differs in that there is no "final consumption" of money except through export or hoarding which Locke finds inconsequential. Money is the "universal commodity," which means that it is constantly accepted and offered in exchange and its vent is not subject to variation (at least not from changes in tastes, the major source of the change in vent of most goods). It should be possible, then, to calculate the vent, or the quickness of circulation, of money to estimate how great a quantity of money is actually needed to drive a certain level of trade. This is precisely what he attempts to do.

Locke goes about calculating how much money is needed to drive the trade by estimating the amount of money each different income group needs to complete its transactions.[67] Laborers are paid once a week, so one-fiftieth of their yearly wage is a good approximation of how much money will be needed in the hands of the laborers and those who pay them. Rents generally come due twice a year, and the money which is used to pay the rent is either saved up from the sale of commodities over some period of time, say three months, or else borrowed from a creditor to be paid back within three months, which means that an amount of money equivalent to the amount of rent will "lye still" for at least a three-month interval. This means that at least one-quarter of the yearly value of rents will be needed in cash to pay rents. Obviously, Locke is describing neither a simple income velocity nor a transactions velocity, but some mixture of the two.[68] While his treatment of day laborers is consistent with income velocity, his treatment of rents is not. If this were a statement of simple income velocity, he would have estimated the amount of cash necessarily in the hands of the rentor or rentee to be half rather than one-quarter of the yearly income from land. Instead, Locke was trying to estimate the time it took for the tenant to save up the money for his rent, the money coming from the selling of his produce. The longer the money "lay dead," the more was needed to drive that portion of the trade. Locke does conclude that where communications are poor, "in the country," more like one-half the total yearly value of rents would really be "necessarily employed in the paying of rents,"[69] but this is not general. In a similar vein, he goes on to estimate how much money will be needed to serve the transactions habits of "brokers" (merchants) and tradesmen, coming out with the conclusion that brokers need at least one-twentieth of their yearly returns to transact their business. All in all, Locke estimates that a country needs one-fiftieth of the value of wages, one-fourth of rents, and one-twentieth of brokers' yearly returns, or, "to put it beyond exception low enough, it cannot be imagined that less than one moiety of this, i.e., less than one-hundredth part of the labourer's yearly wages, one-eighth part of the landholder's yearly revenue, and one-fortieth part of the broker's yearly returns, in ready money, can be enough to move the several wheels of trade, and keep up commerce, in that life and thriving posture it should be."[70] Exactly why he wanted to divide his original estimate by two is not completely clear. It may have been that he believed that credit could make up the rest,[71] or it may have been simply for the reason he gave: He wished to err on the side of underestimation rather than on the side of overestimation.

Locke made it clear that in his estimations of the needed money supply he was not interested in how much any one individual held for any length of time, "for that at other times may be distributed into other hands, and serve other parts of trade: but how much money is necessary to be in each man's hands all the year round, taking one time with another, i.e., having three hundred pounds in his hand one month, is to be reckoned as one hundred pounds in his hand three months."[72] He was thus trying to estimate an average amount for an average time period. He noted that the economy would be better off if the quickness of circulation could be increased because less money then would be needed to drive the trade, and he implied that a fixed amount of money could support a greater volume of transactions when velocity increased.[73] Unfortunately, he never reached the stated conclusion that an increase in the velocity of money could also raise the price level with a fixed amount of output.

## LOCKE'S SYSTEM

To call Locke's theory a quantity theory of money, no matter what the precedent, is to tell only half the story. Although it is obvious that Locke had a clear understanding of the proportional relationship between the quantity of money and the value of money (the price level) and knew how velocity would affect the variables in the quantity equation, his theory of money was really only part of his more general value theory. While changes in the value of money are brought about by changes in the quantity of money available, Locke is quick to point out that often what appears to be an alteration in the value of money actually reflects a change in the real value of goods. Money is the "standing measure of the falling and rising value of other things in reference to one another,"[74] but a change in its value can be instigated by a change in either real values or money values.

> Thus it comes to pass, that there is no manner of settled proportion between the value of an ounce of silver and any other commodity: for either varying its quantity in that country, or the commodity changing its quantity in proportion to its vent, their respective values change, i.e., less of one will barter for more of the other: though, in the ordinary way of speaking, it is only said, that the price of the commodity, not of the money, is changed.[75]

If we now take all the elements of Locke's theory together, what emerges is a single, consistent theory of the determination of all prices as a result of changing proportions. First, he states that the price of any good (including money) is directly proportional to the vent of the good and inversely proportional to its quantity. This proportion of vent to quantity "is actually *a determinant*" of the exchange value of the good in terms of the other goods in the society. All goods, then, have prices that reflect the proportionality of their vent to their quantity relative to those of all other goods in the economy. This establishes the relative value of the goods (when two goods exchange for each other, an exchange of equal values has taken place). One of these goods is singled out as the measure of the changes in these relative values, a numeraire. It then takes on the peculiar characteristic of being readily acceptable in exchange for all goods and so develops a constant vent. Its quantity alone determines its relative value, which is the same as the absolute price level of all other goods for which it exchanges. Money becomes the counterbalance to all the goods, the universal commodity by which we express the relative values of all other commodities. The commodity nature of money interferes with its function as a measure of relative value because its own relative value can change and obscure the actual changes in the relative value of commodities. Therefore, the proportion of the money supply to the number of goods offered for sale is extremely important.

When considered as a whole, Locke's theory of value appears to be more a system for explaining the behavior of the economy than simply a theory of price. He describes the determination of relative prices as a set of proportions between quantities offered for sale and quantities buyers are willing to buy, and the determination of absolute prices as the proportion of the money supply to the transactions completed. His discussion of the velocity of circulation indicates both that he understood how money facilitates circulation of goods and services throughout an economy and that he understood the dual role of each person as producer and consumer. He has no more than a dim perception of the role of price in allocating resources efficiently, but he certainly describes the circular flow of goods and money throughout an economy with price as the facilitator of the flow.[76] His tool for explaining this system is a set of proportions which, although not adequate for the job he makes it do, nevertheless lends an aura of scientific precision to his work in that scientific age. His model is limited in explanatory powers yet he uses it to its best advantage to explain the behavior of many economic variables. How he does this is the subject of the next chapter.

# THREE

# The Wealth of the Nation

JOHN LOCKE PUBLISHED his economic essays in the 1690s, toward the end of the mercantilist era in economic thought, a fact that has led to his often being classified as a mercantilist.[1] Although there are some grounds for this assessment, in a very crucial sense it is untenable, since what Locke shared with this group of writers was by no means the most characteristic part of his work.

Although there is some disagreement as to whether or not mercantilism can be considered a distinct school of economic thought, some unifying elements can be found in the ideas of these widely divergent pamphleteers.[2] Specifically, they shared a common aim: a strong Britain in both the economic and the political senses, and although this aim does not make them unique among economists, they coupled it with the belief that the only way Britain could achieve it was if other nations grew correspondingly weak. They also shared a common estimate of the means of achieving this aim: by maintaining a large stock of precious metals through consistent export surpluses in foreign trade, in the belief that a constant inflow of specie would lead to low interest rates, increased trade, increased capital stock, high employment, and high prices, all vital to their conception of a healthy economy.[3]

If these were the only unifying characteristics of mercantilism, it would not be unreasonable to classify Locke with this group. He certainly shared their nationalistic goals and purpose in writing: he believed his first duty was to secure the fortune of England in what he saw as a zero-sum game of world trade. As for the policies which he believed would achieve his goal of British economic strength, they too have something in common with a large proportion of seventeenth-century mercantilists. He shared their belief in the necessity of specie inflows from world trade and the beneficial effects of these inflows on domestic trade. In addition, if he did not exactly confuse the concepts of money and of capital, he followed the mercantilist practice of calling them by the same name and so developed a monetary theory of interest typical of the mercantilists. And although his ideas on the role of interest in the economy were contrary to what some mercantilist writers thought, there were still others who agreed with him, although perhaps for slightly different reasons.[4] In spite of all these similarities between Locke and the mercantilists, however, there is one area of difference so great that it alone is sufficient to prevent Locke from being included in the group. That area is their respective approaches to economic inquiry.

The mercantilists were practical men who wrote about specific problems on the basis of their observations of the economy. They were usually businessmen who understood how national policy affected their private interests and tried to defend these interests in their tracts. Often their arguments were incorrect, but more often they were incomplete, limited by the one-sided approach they took to the problems with which they concerned themselves. Although the best of them had sophisticated ideas about the relationship between important economic variables like the interest rate, the supply of money, the price level, and the level of trade, few of them rose above mere assertion with little or no theoretical support. This nontheoretical approach to economics can be considered a defining characteristic of mercantilism.

Toward the end of the seventeenth century, this disjointed and often biased approach to economic problems began to yield to the general trend to organize scientific discoveries around a few basic principles, and writers on economic questions began to emerge in England who were distinctly non-mercantilist in this respect. One of the first, Sir William Petty, was even more than John Locke a creature of the new science of experimentation and measurement, and it was in this spirit that he set out to investigate the economic problems of the day.[5] For his "method," Petty vowed to forego the use of "comparative and superlative words and intellectual arguments," and limit himself to expressions "in terms of number, weight or measure; to use only arguments of sense, and to consider only such causes as have visible foundations in nature; leaving those that depend upon mutable minds, opinions, appetites, and passions of particular men, to the consideration of others."[6] The result was that he was one of the first men to adopt a statistical approach to the examination of economic phenomena.[7] However, Petty still dealt with each problem separately, and produced, instead of a unified system of economic thought, a collection of essays using a scientific approach to economic problems.[8] That a consistent theory does seem to emerge from his disparate writings is more a result ultimately of the logic of his mind than of any conscious attempt on his part to produce such a theory.

Another writer of the seventeenth century who attempted to create a system of economic thought (and to a large degree succeeded) was Dudley North. North was a merchant with little formal education and even less scientific training, yet he was so much a man of his age, and the age was so highly scientific, that with only his specialized talent for trade to guide him he was able to formalize many of the economic notions prevalent in his day into a deductive system which was based on human behavior for its motivation and operation. William Letwin goes so far as to call him the first economic theorist to base his policy conclusions entirely on a deductive system, and attributes to him the first equilibrium model of economic behavior.[9] North published his *Discourses upon Trade* within a year of Locke's *Some Considerations,* but he was almost completely without influence on the development of economic thought.

If Locke must be classified with either the mercantilist-practitioners or the scientist-theorists, there is no doubt that he belongs in the latter camp rather than in the former. Although his writings on economics were intended in the mercantilist tradition to be useful in attacking a government policy, his habit of thinking would not allow him to stop with superficial reasons or current clichés to explain his position. Although he agreed with some currently popular conclusions on the subjects of money and foreign trade, he found it necessary to construct a system upon which to found these conclusions. As a result, Locke like Petty before him, and North a few years after him, can be regarded as a systematizer of economic thought. This is easily seen by examining the so-called mercantilist aspect of his writing: his ideas on interest, rents, and foreign trade.

It was explained in the preceding chapter that the underlying structure for Locke's conclusions was a model of price determination depending upon the rational economic behavior of demanders and suppliers which extended to all commodities, including the peculiar case of the money commodity. Locke's system was essentially microeconomic in that it dealt with individual units such as suppliers, consumers, farmers, laborers, traders, and manufacturers. Within this microeconomic system, however, there were certain prices which were vital to the economic well-being of the economy as a whole: the price of money (its purchasing power), the price of the hire of money (the interest rate), the rent of land, and the price of foreign commodities compared with the foreign price of domestic commodities (or the terms of trade). Each of these prices was important in determining the level of trade and the level of income in the economy, upon which in turn depended the prosperity of the nation. The uniqueness of Locke's approach was that he asked the macroeconomic question, What will enrich the nation as a whole? and he answered it with the aid of his microeconomic apparatus. He had one consistent theory to encompass all economic behavior, into which he wove pieces drawn from the existing attitudes of his time. If he failed from time to time to make a crucial distinction or draw an obvious conclusion, the fault was that the structure of his theory could not always accommodate the situations he wanted to explain.

In Locke's macroeconomic scheme, the one price which he considered to be the most important to the maintenance of prosperity was the rate of interest. It was for this reason that he wrote his essay to persuade Parliament not to legislate a lower legal rate of interest. He disagreed with the view of many of his contemporaries who insisted that a low rate of interest was necessary for prosperity,[10] and to prove his argument he analyzed to his own satisfaction all the causes and effects of interest rates in general. From this he developed his general theory of what caused prosperity and wealth. It is fruitful, then, to begin analyzing Locke's macroeconomic theories by examining his theory of the determination and function of the interest rate in the economy.

## THE RATE OF INTEREST

Locke was writing in an era in which interest-taking was an accepted commercial practice, but one that was still viewed with the suspicious eye of lingering Scholasticism.[11] Even in the seventeenth century, usury was held suspect by clergy and laity alike, a circumstance which probably induced Locke to try to establish the moral neutrality of interest. Locke made use of his theory of the origin of society, a theory based on natural law, to explain why money should yield a return.[12]

In the state of nature, the condition which Locke postulates existed before men entered into a civil society, each person had access to an unlimited store of natural resources from which he could appropriate, through his own efforts, whatever he wanted and could make use of without waste. Since to waste anything was the only way a man could forfeit his right to his property and the most valuable things in life were also the most perishable, no one had any reason or any means to try to accumulate a store of private wealth. As a result, no private fortunes could be built, and each man had an equal chance to use his skill to acquire nature's gifts. Once men agreed to put an imaginary value on gold and silver, however, and use them as money, men were provided at once with a means and a reason to try to accumulate wealth, and personal fortunes began to arise. Without the existence of money, a more industrious person would no doubt be better clothed and better fed than his less industrious neighbors; but with the existence of a store of value, more industrious men could increase this disparity of economic well-being and pass it on to their children, who could further augment the family fortune. The result would be an unequal distribution of wealth.

Locke reasoned that eventually all land would become private property, making it no longer possible for a newcomer to "homestead" in the wilderness and thus build up his fortune in the same manner as those who came before him. He would still be able to use his own labor, but now the resources with which to mix his labor would have to come from someone who already owned them; the resources would have to be either bought or borrowed from someone who had more than he could use himself and who was willing to convert a portion of his stored wealth into money. Locke did not consider this to be unjust, however, because although the original settlers in the state of nature had the advantage of starting with free resources, presumably they improved upon them when they established their ownership rights, enabling the rentee to benefit from the improvement. If the newcomer were to buy the resources from their owner he would have to pay a price equal to their improved value, and if instead he decided merely to rent the use of the resources he would have to compensate the owner in proportion to the profit he was making from their use. The payment for borrowing the use of another man's land is what Locke called "rent," and the payment for borrowing the use of another man's money is what Locke called "interest."[13]

Just as Locke had given a fundamental reason for why people want goods (because of their intrinsic value), so he gave a fundamental reason for the existence of a rate of interest—an unequal distribution of wealth. To the question, Why do men pay use? he answers, "for the same reason... as the tenant pays rent for your land."[14] Both land and money are unequally distributed, so both can yield a return when lent out. Rather than being cause for moral condemnation as the Scholastics argued, it is a perfectly equitable practice growing out of the voluntary actions of human beings obeying natural law. It hurts no one, since interest is a payment for receiving the benefit of another man's wealth: "he that has skill in traffic, but has not money enough to exercise it, has not only reason to borrow money to drive his trade, and get a livelihood; but as much reason to pay use for that money; as he, who having skill in husbandry but no land of his own to employ it in, has not only reason to rent land, but to pay money for the use of it."[15] Interest-taking is no more or no less moral than accepting rent, both of which have the advantage of providing gain for both the borrower and the lender. Although this account of the origin of interest is nothing more than a sidelight to his analysis and occupies little space relative to the size of his whole essay, it accurately reflects Locke's attitude toward the economic problem he is analyzing: interest-taking is natural and no less moral than any other kind of economic activity.[16]

Once it is established that interest is nothing more than a

premium paid for the use of someone else's property, it next becomes important to establish why money is productive of such a return. It has already been noted that money has a double value in Locke's system: a value in use and a value in exchange. Money has value in exchange because it aids in the transaction of sales, and this value is measured by the number of goods which will exchange for it. Money has value in use because of its ability to bring in an income for those who lend it out. This value is measured by the rate people will pay for its use, the rate of interest. Although he has so far given a superficial reason why people borrow money, which amounts to saying they will borrow it because they do not have enough, now he must give a reason why people are willing to pay a return for the use of money they need. Locke's answer to why money, ''a barren thing,'' should be able to bring a return to its owner by transferring ''that profit, that was the reward of one man's labour, into another man's pocket''[17] revolves around his partially formed theory of capital.

Money brings in a return first of all because it is needed to engage in money-making activities. The producer of manufactured articles needs money to pay his workers and to buy his raw materials, the farmer to buy supplies and to pay his workers, the shipper to stock his ship for what he hopes will be a lucrative voyage, the merchant to purchase inventories of goods he will offer for sale.[18] In other words, Locke is describing the need for money capital or circulating capital in order to engage in production for a profit. He is quite explicit about why money capital is necessary to the carrying on of business; money is needed by the producer to bridge the time gap from the beginning of a productive endeavor to when the finished product is ready for sale.

> Every man must have at least so much money, or so timely recruits, as may in hand, or in a short distance of time, satisfy his creditor who supplies him with the necessaries of life, or of his trade. For nobody has any

longer these necessary supplies, then he has money, or credit, which is nothing else but an assurance of money, in some short time. So that it is requisite to trade, that there should be so much money as to keep up the landholder's, labourer's, and broker's credit.[19]

Here money capital is needed to pay creditors who supply the raw materials of trade, and the longer the time it takes for a man to collect his receipts, the more money capital is needed to run a business.[20]

While Locke clearly understands the role of money capital in business activity, he does not show any understanding of the relationship between money capital and real capital. The concept of real capital was not unknown to him, however, since in the *Second Treatise* Locke describes the advantages to an economy of having a stock of real capital, even though he never identifies it as such. In the *Second Treatise,* Locke implies that capital is really the product of past labor which combines with current labor to increase its productivity. In one passage, he describes the production of bread as consisting of many stages of production each of which adds present labor ("human industry") to the product of past labor. The great number of these stages of production Locke takes to be a sign of economic development because of the increased value of the raw materials at each state, as in the production of bread:

> For 'tis not barely the plough-man's pains, the reaper's and thresher's toil, and the baker's sweat, is to be counted into the bread we eat; the labour of those who broke the oxen, who digged and wrought the iron and stones, who felled and framed the timber imployed about the plough, mill, oven, or any other utensils, which are a vast number, requisite to this corn, from its being seed to be sown to its being made bread, must all be charged on the account of labour, and received as an effect of that: Nature and

the earth furnish only the almost worthless materials,
as in themselves. 'Twould be a strange catalogue of
things, that industry provided and made use of,
about every loaf of bread, before it came to our use,
if we could trace them; Iron, wood, leather, bark,
timber, stone, bricks, coals, lime, cloth, dying-drugs,
pitch, tar masts, ropes, and all the materials made
use of in the ship, that brought any of the commodities made use of by any of the workmen, to any part
of the work, all which, 'twould be almost impossible,
at least too long, to reckon up.[21]

Here it seems that Locke's understanding of capital is more
classical than neoclassical, since he never identifies capital as a
productive input apart from labor. In some respects, however, his whole view of the production process differs even
from the classical view with which it has been linked. For
Locke the only productive element in the creation of goods
and services is the labor that goes into them: land is a passive
pool of resources which must be acted upon by labor to
produce anything of value (notice the similarity to Petty
here). It takes conscious human industry to produce anything
valuable, and even though Locke talks in his theory of property about labor being "joined" to land to create property, it
is not a mechanistic joining, but the creative act of an individual.[22] Once man expends labor upon resources, he produces valuable goods, some of which are intermediate goods
(or "goods in process," to use Hayek's terminology) that
increase the value of output at later stages of production.
These intermediate goods form the capital stock of the economy. According to this interpretation of Locke's description
of capital, his understanding of the phenomenon is more
closely related to the later Austrian school than to either the
classical or the neoclassical economists.

Given that Locke did understand real capital as intermediate "goods in process," and given his understanding of
money capital evidenced in *Some Considerations,* we can

construct a link between the two and between capital and interest which Locke himself failed to provide. Labor acts upon natural resources to create valuable commodities, some of which are intermediate goods. The producers of these goods sell them and save some of the money they receive for them. This money forms what Locke calls "stock." This money capital which represents the savings of the lender can then be lent out to a commercial borrower who will use money capital to purchase already produced intermediate goods to enable him to produce and sell his final product. The lender requires a premium or interest payment to induce him to take the risk of lending out his hard-earned money, while the borrower is willing to pay such a premium or rate of interest because he can use this money capital to make a profit from his business. Locke does not go on from there, however, to show any regular relationship between the rate of interest and the rate of profit.[23]

Locke has been charged in the literature with failing to understand the concept of capital and/or with making no distinction between money and capital.[24] Both these charges are unduly harsh, yet one can readily see how a reader would be led to such a conclusion. Where Locke's theory of capital suffers is that he uses the same word to represent both the medium of exchange and circulating capital. When he speaks of a proportion of money needed to drive a given level of trade, sometimes he is referring to the velocity of circulation of money as the medium of exchange, and sometimes he means that a given level of trade needs some proportion of money capital to support it: only the context can show which is which. The problem with interpreting Locke on this issue is that he understood and described the two separate phenomena, money as a medium of exchange and money capital necessary to invest in real capital, but he called them by the same name. As far as he was concerned, both were attributes of the same commodity, precious metals, which happened to serve two functions in economic life. Unfortunately, the presentation of capital in this form made it difficult for him to keep the two values of money separate in his analyses, and this leaves his use of the different functions of money open to confusion.[25]

Just as money in exchange was a commodity which had a price determined in the same way as any other price, so money in use also had a price subject to the same laws of determination as any other good. This rate of interest, "the price of the hire of money," depended on the quantity of money in proportion to its vent. Locke's clear and detailed description of the determinants of both the quantity and the vent of money in use is the most involved application of his value theory to a specific problem.

On the demand side, Locke's major argument was that men borrow only for the sake of making a profit, and as long as a profit can be made on the enterprise they will be willing to pay a premium for the use of money: "It is to be remembered, that no man borrows money, or pays use, out of mere pleasure: 'tis the want of money drives men to that trouble and charge of borrowing; and proportionably to this want, so will everyone have it, whatever price it cost him."[26] As long as the profit exceeds the cost of borrowing, men will borrow money. Traders will "purchase money lent to them, at what rate so ever their occasion shall make it necessary for them to have."[27] Locke does not describe an inverse price–quantity–demand relationship where men borrow more at lower rates of interest and less at higher ones. He states only that how much they are willing to pay in interest is "proportionable" to their want, with no indication of how or if this relates to changes in the rate of interest.

On the supply side, those who lend out money do so in order to get a return, but lending involves a risk to the lender that he may not be paid back. The greater the risk, the higher must be the interest rate to compensate for the risk. If the reward is fixed (as it would be with an established legal interest rate), the aim of the lender then becomes to minimize his risk, which will affect the distribution of loanable funds among borrowers. More will flow into the relatively safe hands of bankers and less into the small, high risk, personal enterprises. At very low rates, minimizing risk will also mean a reduction in the amount of money lent out, especially when the loans are from foreign lenders: "Now it cannot be rationally expected, but that where the venture is great, and the gains small, (as it is in lending in England upon low interest) many will choose rather to hoard up their money, than venture it abroad on such terms."[28] Clearly, Locke sees a direct relationship between rates of interest and the quantity of money supplied.[29]

Just as any other price is formed by the interaction of demanders and suppliers of the good in question, the rate of interest is determined by the interaction of the demanders and suppliers of money in use. When money is in short supply, given some level of demand, the interest rate rises, so that if there were "a million of money in England. . . . But if two millions were necessary to carry on the trade, there would be a million wanting, and the price of money would be raised."[30] Interest will rise "when money is little in proportion to the trade of a country."[31] On the other hand, given a certain quantity of money, demand for it alone sets the price.[32] As in his general price theory, Locke shows price changes by varying only one variable at a time and holding everything else constant.

This rate of interest, which was the result of the interactions between the borrowers and the lenders, was only one of three different rates he described, the one he called the market rate. The other two rates were the legal and the natural rates. The legal rate was the one set by Parliament to establish a fair rate for debts "where contract has not settled it between the parties."[33] It was a juridical standard for the awarding of damages, which ideally should reflect the market rate of interest. The natural rate of interest, on the other hand, was a little more complex: It was, in Locke's words, "that rate of money which the present scarcity of it makes it naturally at, upon an equal distribution of it."[34] Under normal conditions, when money is evenly distributed throughout the kingdom, the natural rate and the market rate will be identical, but if something allows a small group of lenders to monopolize the money capital to be lent out, they can drive the market rate higher than it would otherwise be. The natural rate is, then, actually the competitive market rate where no one person or group has control over any portion of the market. If a monopoly does get control, Locke argued that a set legal rate would be necessary to prevent "extortion and oppression" by the monopolist, assuming that the legal rate was set very close to the natural rate of interest.[35]

Locke was insistent about how monopoly power could drive up the rate of interest. If "bankers and scriveners, and other such expert brokers, who [are] skilled in the arts of putting out money"[36] gain a monopoly, "they could be content to have more money lie dead by them, than now,...by which means there would be less money stirring in trade, and greater scarcity, which would raise upon the borrower by this monopoly."[37] By restricting supply, the monopolist could drive up the price and increase his profits. Although he had no concept of an optimal price which would maximize monopoly profits, he realized that under monopoly, interest would be higher than the natural price for money, and profits greater for the "bankers and scriveners" who lent it out, while the public would suffer as a result of a lack of money for trade. These consequences were not limited to banking monopolies, but were true of all markets where a group of producers was able to "engross" a large proportion of the supply, a fact which made Locke share the common mercantilist distrust of monopoly privilege.[38]

If we can generalize from this account, it would appear that Locke's idea of a natural price was far different from that of either Petty or Smith. Petty, and later Smith, set up theories in which natural price was the price which would in the long run tend to approach the cost of production of a commodity, in much the same way as Marshall's long-run price theory. They described this price in opposition to the market price, which would fluctuate according to short-run changes in supply and demand. Locke's natural price, on the other hand, had nothing to do with costs of production, but instead depended entirely upon the relatively equal distribution of the output among suppliers for its determination. If the supply is widely distributed among the sellers, no one seller will be able to affect the price significantly, and more consumers will get a chance to consume the product. In some ways, this account of natural price is also a forerunner of Marshall's competitive price with its large number of sellers, but with the emphasis placed on the market conditions rather than the underlying cost structure. If one looks back instead of forward, however, Locke's natural price is reminiscent of Aristotle's just exchange in which neither party gets an excess gain so long as bargaining among equals takes place.[39]

Since interest was a price determined by the voluntary actions of men, Locke believed that the legal rate should not diverge from the natural rate of interest. In fact, he argued that any attempt to set the legal rate below the rate dictated by the market was not only undesirable but, in the end, impossible. Interest was a price like any other price, and " 'Tis in vain, therefore, to go about effectually to reduce the price of interest by law; and you may as rationally hope to set a fixed rate upon the hire of houses, or ships, as of money."[40] A law designed to reduce the rate of interest to the borrower below the market rate would be less than useless, because it would be almost universally circumvented and the cost of the circumvention would fall upon the borrower. Regardless of the law, the market would have its way, and "this will be the result of all such attempts, that experience will show that the price of things will not be regulated by laws, though the endeavors after it will be sure to prejudice and inconvenience trade, and put your affairs out of order."[41] If the present state of profitability warrants a higher interest rate, borrowers will not hesitate to borrow at that rate, and lenders will manage to find ways of accepting the higher rate: "the skillful...will always so manage it, as to avoid the prohibition of your law, and keep out of its penalty, do what you can."[42] The only result will be "that your act, at best, will serve only to increase the arts of lending, but not at all lessen the charge of the borrower."[43] In fact, the law will most probably work to cause the exact opposite result from the one that is desired: borrowers will end up paying higher rates of interest and be obliged to go to more trouble to secure a loan.

Locke believed that it was best for the trade of the nation if direct lending took place between individual lenders and private entrepreneurs. Since small enterprises were spread out all through the country and not limited just to the large financial centers like London, it would be advantageous to have loanable funds evenly distributed throughout the country. This would minimize the cost of lending by eliminating middlemen (a group which Locke, like many of his mercantilist predecessors, thought the country could do without), and it would reduce the "circuit" which money would have to travel (i.e., reduce transactions costs). These direct transactions, in rural areas, however, were usually high-risk loans and demanded that a higher rate of interest go to the lender than a safer transaction would warrant. If the legal rate were held below the natural rate, lenders would not find it profitable to lend directly to borrowers "in the country," but would rather minimize risk by giving their money to the bankers who would guarantee it on short notice. Bankers, however, "skilled in the arts of putting out money according to the true and natural value," would use their skill to get the market rate regardless of the law.[44] In addition, since they would have most of the loanable funds in England concentrated in their hands, they would gain a monopoly and force up the market rate above the natural rate by two means: first by restricting supply (engrossing), and second by an increase in their supply function because of the increased risk of getting caught lending at a higher than legal rate. The final result is that the law designed to lower the interest rate to the borrowers will cause private individuals to adjust their portfolios away from high-risk borrowers to low-risk banks, allowing the banks to achieve a monopoly and increase the cost of borrowing to an even higher level than was prevalent before the law was passed.[45]

Although these were the consequences that would undoubtedly follow the passage of the interest law, Locke argued that even if a law to lower the rate of interest from six to four per cent were actually passed and obeyed, the major consequence would be a redistribution of income and a reduction in the quantity of money available for lending, rather than an increased level of trade resulting from reduced costs of production, as the advocates of the law believed. The redistribution of income would be most felt by "widows, orphans, and all those who have their estates in money," who would have the value of their estates reduced by one-third.[46] And, while people living on the income of their money, those "who are least capable of taking care of themselves," would lose, there would be a gain to the "borrowing merchant" who would be able to keep more of his profit. "For if he borrows at four percent., and his return be twelve percent., he will have eight percent., and the lender four: whereas now they divide the profit equally at six percent."[47] This assumes that the rate of investment will remain the same at both rates of interest, if both the borrower and lender are Englishmen, there will be no net gain to England, and therefore no good reason to impose the interest rate reduction. "Private men's interests ought not thus to be neglected, nor sacrificed to anything but the manifest advantage of the public."[48] In addition to the redistribution of income, the second effect would be a reduction in the amount of money available to be lent out, because the moneyed man will be discouraged from lending ''at such a disproportion of profit to risque.''[49] He will lend out less, creating a shortage of money, so that the final result will be a decrease in the level of trade rather than an increase in it.

A law reducing the rate of interest, then, will have only bad effects. If interest rates are held artificially low, bankers will find ways to get around the law, charge the going rate for money, and pass the cost of avoiding the law on to the borrower. If the law were strictly enforced, the only result would be a reduction in the quantity of money lent out, which would further enhance the discrepancy between the legal and the market rate of interest. In either case, the nation would lose, first from an increased market rate of interest which would increase the cost and reduce the profits from trade, and second from a reduction in the total volume of trade possible. While the first result is obvious, the second is not and needs a little more explanation.

## THE VOLUME OF TRADE

The connection between the rate of interest, the quantity of money in circulation, and the total volume of trade is not an easy one to unravel. On the surface, Locke seems to be saying that money is needed for trade; the more money, the more trade that can be carried on, and the lower the rate of interest, the more money that will be available. The level of trade, further, is proportional to the amount of money in circulation. If this were the extent of his argument, he would seem to have been supporting the mercantilist proclivity for low interest rates, a bias he took pains to disagree with. Josiah Child had argued that low interest would be beneficial to the country since it would make profits high and encourage trade. Locke, however, countered this argument by maintaining that low interest rates were not necessarily a cause of prosperity, just as high interest rates were not necessarily a detriment to it. In fact, he claimed that England was never so well off as it was during a time when the rate of interest was as high as eight or ten per cent: "I will not say high interest was the cause of it. For I rather think that our thriving trade was the cause of high interest, everyone craving money to employ in a profitable commerce. But, this I think, I may reasonably infer from it, that lowering of interest is not a sure way to improve either our trade or wealth."[50] Since the rate of interest depends both on supply and demand, the rate of interest alone is not enough to indicate the state of prosperity of the economy. Prosperity could be reflected either in interest rates that are high because of a great demand for money to carry on trade, or in interest rates that are low because there is plenty of money to drive and increase the trade of the nation. As Vickers[51] points out, contrary to accepted mercantilist opinion, Locke regarded interest as an effect and not a cause of general economic conditions.[52] The intentions of borrowers and lenders determine these conditions, and the real way to increased prosperity for the nation was to keep the interest rate free to reflect them. That is, the real inhibitor of trade was not a high interest rate, but a disequilibrium rate that created a shortage of money.[53]

Hecksher has maintained that if Locke had substituted the phrase *loanable funds* for the word *money* whenever he discussed the determination of the interest rate, his argument would have been faultless.[54] In fact, we have already seen that Locke had a concept of capital stock from which money that was loaned out at interest was taken. A problem with Hecksher's interpretation arises, however, in the context of Locke's description of the proportion of money needed to drive the trade. After establishing that an artificially low interest rate will reduce the amount of lending and hinder trade, Locke then shows that there is some proportion of money necessary to support a given level of trade. But, "the necessity therefore of a proportion of money to trade, depends on money not as counters, for the reckoning may be kept, or transferred by writing; but on money as a pledge,...because a law cannot give to bills that intrinsic value which the universal consent of mankind has annexed to silver and gold."[55] In other words, the necessity of a proportion of money to trade is the necessity of an exchange medium to trade, and this exchange medium is used by producers as money capital (or money in use) and by consumers as purchasing power (money in exchange). Again, he emphasizes the two separate functions of the single commodity, money.

What Locke seems to be describing here is a circular flow between producers and consumers, where the level of trade can be measured either by the expenditure by consumers on goods and services, or by the amounts producers pay out in costs of production. A given quantity of money can support a given level of trade, and changes in the quantity of money will be reflected in changes both in the price level and in the rate of interest, wages, and rents. Furthermore, it is only through the medium of the quantity of money that interest rates can have any effect on prices.

There was a common belief in Locke's day that lowering the interest rate would somehow "raise the value of money," a belief which gave Locke the title to his 1692 essay and which was the starting point for his criticism of the proposed legislation on interest. Locke maintained that interest and the value of money in exchange were two separate things, and depended upon different determinants for their value. A change in the interest rate would have no immediate effect on prices because

> the fall therefore or rise of interest, making immediately by its change neither more nor less land, money; or any sort of commodity in England, than there was before, alters not at all the value of money, in reference to commodities. Because the measure of that is only the quantity and vent, which are not immediately changed by the change of interest.[56]

There is only one way in which a change in the rate of interest can affect the level of prices: "So far as the change of interest conduces in trade to the bringing in or carrying out of money or commodities and so in time to the varying their proportions here in England from what it was before, so far the change of interest as all other things that promote or hinder trade may alter the value of money, in reference to commodities.''[57] If prices rise or fall, the market rate of interest will not be directly affected, and if the interest rate changes, there will be no immediate effect on the price level; lowering the interest rate does not cause the value of money to rise. An artificially lowered interest rate may cause less money to be loaned out, but this has no immediate effect on prices. It is only when money is either brought into or carried out of the country that a change in the rate of interest will change the price level, and that can occur only when there are ramifications in the foreign trade sector of the economy.

Locke was in favor of the mercantilist policy of having an inflow of precious metals (especially silver, which was coined in small enough denominations to be used as the primary money commodity), and early in his essay he pointed out that there were only two ways in which England could achieve this purpose: through conquest and through trade. Of the two, trade was by far the more efficient.[58] As a result, foreign trade theory played an important part in Locke's analysis of what causes a wealthy England. Locke was living in a country that made a great proportion of its living by trading with other nations, and he had been involved in politics long enough to realize that the stronger that position, the better off the country would be both economically and militarily. England relied on her exports to bring in foreign exchange, and anything that hurt her relative position in world markets could only reduce the flow of gold and silver into England. It is no wonder that Locke's primary concern was with a strong trading position and high prices for English exports.

FOREIGN TRADE

Locke's primary assumption was that in order to be an effective competitor in the world market and thus be strong and prosperous, a country needs a proportion of the world's money supply equal to its proportion of total world trade. Although a country existing in isolation could have any quantity of money to drive its trade, the price level simply adjusting to the money supply, if it trades with other nations it cannot afford that luxury: it must have at least enough money to keep its prices as high as those of its competitors.[59] Its failure to maintain prices equivalent to world prices would lead to a whole series of consequences which would end by weakening it economically and politically. If silver were lacking and production were to remain constant, according to Locke's quantity theory, prices would fall, causing domestic products to be sold cheap in world markets and foreign products to be more expensive in the domestic market. This would make no difference to domestic traders, since all prices at home are assumed to fall, but importers of foreign goods would be forced to pay for the relatively high priced foreign commodities with their domestically more valuable gold, and consequently would suffer a loss of profits, an important consideration for a small island kingdom which depended greatly on international trade.[60]

Instead of taking the next step in reasoning out a price-specie-flow mechanism and showing that the fall in prices would increase exports and increase the flow of gold into England once again, as Hume did in the next century, Locke preferred to point out the effects in terms of the labor supply: "It endangers the drawing away our people, both handicrafts, mariners, and soldiers, who are apt to go where the pay is best, which will always be where there is greatest plenty of money."[61] Locke seems not to have even considered the possibility that this was in any way a reversible process that would bring about an automatic adjustment. Other than sheer lack of insight, which is always a possibility, one reason for Locke's failure to describe a self-regulating equilibrium might have been that he considered England's trading position to be such that the sum of the elasticity of demand for her imports and exports was less than one, in which case silver would continue to flow out of England as the terms of trade turned against her and further increase the disadvantage of the English traders. Obviously Locke would not have been able to state the problem in this way, but it is an assumption which is consistent with the consequences he describes.[62]

If poverty relative to the rest of the world was the consequence of a low proportion of money to trade, prosperity was the reward of having a high proportion of money to trade and high prices in the world market. Locke seems to have had a bias in favor of high prices for domestic commodities selling on the world market because he believed that this would cause more total revenue to come into England than if domestic commodities "sold cheap."[63] He seems not to have seen the possibility that lower prices might give a competitive advantage to a trading country, and in this respect he retrogressed from the advice of Thomas Mun to sell at high prices ("as high as the traffick will bear") only those goods that England had a monopoly in the manufacture of, while disposing as "cheap as possible" of those for which it had competitors, in order to maximize the revenues gotten from foreign trade.[64] One possible reason is that in his discussions of foreign trade he is more concerned with the relative value of England's domestic money supply than with ways of increasing England's foreign markets, and he fails to make the connection between the two. At any rate, the means to achieve the enviable position of strength and wealth vis-a-vis foreign countries was to maintain a constant inflow of silver by importing fewer commodities than were exported.[65]

Unlike some of his mercantilist contemporaries,[66] Locke did not desire a positive trade balance for the sake of pure accumulation of metals or "riches." He agreed that wealth consisted in an inflow of precious metals, but only because of the commodities which they could purchase. "Gold and silver, though they serve for few, yet they command all the conveniences of life; and therefore in a plenty of them consists riches,''[67] we are told in *Some Considerations,* and soon afterward Locke adds, ''Riches do not consist in having more gold and silver, but in having more in proportion, than the rest of the world, or than our neighbors, whereby we are enabled to procure to ourselves a greater plenty of the conveniences of life.''[68] This indicates very clearly that Locke did not share what Hecksher has called the mercantilist ''disregard of consumption,''[69] although Locke does sometimes sound as if he were more interested in stocks of gold and silver than in the goods they could buy. One such instance is his use of the familiar analogy of the farmer who spends less than he produces, to indicate the proper policy for a country to follow in order to build up a surplus of wealth.[70] Here he postulates that a country is to the world trade as one individual is to the trade of a domestic economy: if an individual can become rich by increasing his stock through spending less then he takes in, the same must be true of a country. The analogy is incomplete, however, because Locke assumed that the increased supply of precious metals would not be uselessly hoarded as by an individual, but instead circulated to the advantage of the economy.[71]

Today textbooks teach that under a gold standard a policy of trying to maintain positive trade balances is futile, because an inflow of gold or silver would lead to an increase in the domestic price level, a fall in domestic exports, and a subsequent outflow of the precious metals. Locke, however, maintained that an inflow of gold would enable an increased volume of trade to be maintained, with an increase in prices being a minor consequence. He has been criticized for failing to apply his quantity theory to international prices, which would have enabled him to develop a price–specie–flow mechanism before Hume in the next century.[72] In fact, he does apply his quantity theory to international prices, but he makes different assumptions about the behavior of the variables. For example:

Supposing then, that we had now in England but half as much money, as we had seven years ago, and yet had still as much yearly product of commodities, as many hands to work them, and as many brokers to disperse them, as before [the money supply decreases by one-half and the output remains the same]; and that the rest of the world we trade with had as much money as they had before, (for 'tis likely they should have more by our moiety shared amongst them) 'tis certain, that either half our rents should not be paid, half our commodities not vented and half our labourers not employed, and so half the trade be clearly lost; or else, that everyone of these must receive but half the money for their commodities and labour they did before, and but half so much as our neighbors do receive for the same labour, and the same natural product at the same time.[73]

His conclusion is that both consequences will occur: domestic prices will fall relative to foreign prices, making foreign imports very expensive; and the wage rate paid to domestic labor will fall as a result. This, he claims, will induce skilled labor to migrate out of England and thereby reduce the productive capacity of the nation. If, on the other hand, the money supply increases through trade surpluses, prices will rise and trade will increase. He was obviously assuming that there was a wealth of investment opportunities in England just waiting to be exploited if only the capital and labor were made available to entrepreneurs. An inflow of money, he believed, would stimulate the employment of these idle resources, while a decrease in the money supply would cause them to continue to lie idle.[74]

While import or export surpluses resulting from changes in international trade patterns will cause a country either to gain or to lose in wealth, Locke understood that not every change in the exchange rate reflects a major change in trading advantage. If a country has a money supply larger than a trading partner's, its price level will be higher and traders will be willing to exchange a promise to pay a certain amount of silver in that country for a lesser amount of silver in the lower-priced country. In other words, bills of exchange of a country with undervalued currency will sell at a premium in terms of the overvalued currency, which will serve to equilibrate the exchange rates between the two countries. Furthermore, there will usually be a small persistent difference in the exchange rates between the two countries which will be equal to the cost of insurance and freight of shipping specie from one country to the other. Locke's description of this phenomenon is a complete and accurate identification of the gold import and export points, which is far superior to discussions in the writings of his contemporaries.[75]

While short-term fluctuations in the money supply within countries can be equalized by changes in the exchange rate, Locke believed that long-term maladjustments due to unbalanced underlying trade patterns would have to be corrected by payments of specie. In such cases, he was scornful of attempts to keep silver in England by forbidding its export. He cites Spain as an example of a country that makes laws forbidding the export of gold without the favorable trade balance to make the policy work: ''Trade fetches it away from that lazy and indigent people, notwithstanding all their artificial and forced contrivances to keep it there. It follows trade, against the rigour of their laws; and their want of foreign commodities makes it openly be carried out at noonday.''[76] His long-term acquaintance with foreign exchange practices enabled him to see the real phenomena upon which exchange variations depended, and so he understood that specie would flow toward the creditor nation regardless of the attempts by the government of the debtor nation to stop it from leaving the country. Unless Spain, for example, produced commodities for export, it could not hope to keep its specie at home. There is only one way in which restricting the export of gold can help keep it at home, and that is by increasing the risk of getting caught, which will increase the cost of exporting gold and thereby raise the gold export point.[77] Other than that, restrictive policies are useless.

In addition to the trade balance, Locke took into account one of the invisible items of the balance of payments, the amount of foreign lending in England.[78] He pointed out that borrowing from a foreign nation resulted in a loss to the nation borrowing equal to the amount of interest paid out, but he also noted that there was a gain to be calculated equal to the amount by which trade was increased because of the borrowing. Implicit in this analysis is the idea of opportunity cost when he says: "Now the kingdom gets or loses by this [borrowing from foreigners] only proportionably (allowing the consumption of foreign commodities to be still the same) as the paying of use to foreigners carries away more or less of our money, than want of money and stopping our trade keeps us from bringing in by hindering our gains."[79] One must calculate the profit in trade before and after the borrowing to see if the increase in borrowing yields a profit greater than the rate of interest. The calculation of this amount can be done only by those who are familiar with the amounts borrowed from foreigners, the interest paid, and the profit received, but Locke's implicit assumption is that the amount is positive. He clearly states that "no country borrows of its neighbors, but where there is need of money for trade,"[80] and "if the merchant's return be more than his use (which 'tis certain it is or else he will not trade)...the kingdom gets by this borrowing, so much as the merchant's gain is above his use."[81] However, Locke also notes that if loans are made for purposes of consumption rather than of engaging in trade, the interest payments are a net loss of specie to the kingdom. In both cases, then, he sees how foreign lending figures into the balance of payments.

## THEORY OF RENT

Another advantage of lowering the interest rate that Locke

claimed was advanced by its advocates had to do with the third part of Locke's macroeconomic trilogy: the rent of land. It was claimed that by lowering the legal rate of interest, the value of land would be increased. Locke believed this to be an absurd claim and went about proving it by analyzing the relationship between land, rent, and the rate of interest.

Locke believed that the basis for wealth in any society was its land and the people who worked upon it.[82] The land-holder was the most valuable member of society and should therefore have his interests looked after before anyone else's.[83] It was in his interest to have his product prices high and his rents correspondingly high, but it was not necessarily in his interest to have interest rates low as was claimed by advocates of the low interest rate bill. Land was capable of bringing in a rent, as was mentioned above, because of the unequal distribution of land which came about when men began to use money.[84] It therefore gained the power to yield an income for the same reason that money could yield an income. And since money and land were alternate forms of investment, it would be logical for the two to yield equal returns: one should expect land to sell at a price that would return the investment in a period of time equal to the recip-rocal of the rate of interest.[85] For example, if the interest rate is ten per cent, £1,000 invested in an annuity would return £100 per year. At this rate, land that rented for £100 per year should sell at ten years' purchase, or an amount equiva-lent to the sum of ten years' worth of rent on the land. According to this reasoning, if the interest rate were to fall and the rent of land remain the same, the value of land would increase in inverse proportion to the amount by which the interest rate had fallen.

Although this argument, Locke agreed, was completely logical on the surface, he maintained that empirical evidence contradicted this result: nowhere in the past had it been the case that land values and interest moved in so exact a relation-ship to one another.[86] Locke believed that upon further reflection, the theoretical evidence would also turn out to be contrary to this assumption. In the first place, it was obvious that the value of land could not be improved by lowering the legal rate of interest, since that would lead only to the host of problems already described in his interest theory. Trade would be hindered; the quantity of money would be reduced, causing the price of commodities to fall; and ultimately the farmer's income would fall along with the prices, the exact opposite of the results predicted by advocates of the lower interest rate. In addition, there were reasons why the rent of land would not follow the natural rate of interest in any predictable pattern, as would at first seem reasonable to assume. First of all, money is a homogeneous commodity and all money will return the same rate of interest, while land is of varying fertility and all land will not return the same rent. Lending money also involves a greater risk than does renting land, because land is fixed and cannot be run off with as money can, and therefore one would expect the rate of interest to be higher then the rent of land.[87] Finally, and most important, Locke's theory of value told him that there would be no easy relationship between the rent of land and interest on money.

Values are determined by the proportion of buyers to sellers, and Locke saw no reason to expect that this proportion will be the same or vary by the same magnitudes in the cases of interest and of rent any more than in those of any other two commodities. "All things that are bought and sold raise and fall their price in proportion as there are more buyers or sellers. . . . This rule holds in land as well as in all other commodities."[88] When demand is high, price tends to rise, and when it is low, price tends to fall. Moreover, Locke believed that land has the special character that when demand is high, supply is low, and vice versa. Demand is high when trade and manufacturing thrive, because profits are high and men are looking for alternative ways of investing their profits, but in that case, land being owned by "that sort of industrious and thriving men, they have neither need, nor will to sell.''[89] The assumption underlying Locke's analysis of the price of land is that land is not simply an alternative investment opportunity whose return will eventually equal the return on other investments. On the contrary, land to Locke was primarily a consumption good which was desired for the style of living it afforded the landowner. He believed that men who were successful in business naturally wanted to purchase an estate to become a member of the landed gentry and to provide an inheritance for their children.[90] But this implies that in industrial areas, when everyone is experiencing high profits, landowning too will be lucrative, since land will be selling at high prices because demand is high and supply is low. But if there is a general falling off in trade in a particular area, or in the country as a whole, prices will fall, rents will go unpaid, and landholders will want to sell but will find few buyers. The result will be that the price of land will fall. Hence, Locke argues that there is no necessary relationship between the rate of interest and the value of land. Furthermore, even if such a relationship existed, lowering the rate of interest would be a policy which "gives the advantage, not to the land holder, but to him that ceases to be so,''[91] whereas the real advantage of the landholder occurs when there are high prices for his products and his rents are great. The proper policy to follow to aid the landowner, then, would be one which would keep specie flowing into the country, the policy that encourages trade through higher prices and profits.[92] According to this criterion, lowering the legal rate of interest to four per cent would be a disaster.

Here again, as in several places before, Locke supported the mercantilist conclusions that a country should try to maintain a favorable balance of trade. As far as he could see, the effects of such a policy would be only beneficial: high prices, high profits, wages, and rents, a high level of aggregate demand, and greater production and trade, all of which are symptoms of a healthy, vigorous economy. He seems to have envisioned no end to the expansionary possibilities of an increasing money supply, possibly because he was arguing on the basis of short-run considerations, and England was suffering from trade deficits and unemployment during the time he was writing.[93]

The title of this chapter, "The Wealth of the Nation," is a conscious paraphrase of the title of Adam Smith's famous book. The slight variation is intended to underscore a major difference between Smith and Locke. Whereas Smith's purpose was to provide a general explanation for the causes of wealth, transcending national boundaries, Locke was interested in providing a prescription for maintaining and increasing the wealth of just one country, England. In this he shared the mercantilist preoccupation. What differentiates Locke from his mercantilist contemporaries, then, was not his conclusions, although some of them did differ from the conventional wisdom, but rather his method of seeking his conclusions. Equipped with his value theory and the quantity theory of money as he understood it as his only tools, he described a policy for achieving the mercantilists' dream of a politically and economically strong kingdom, and yet at the same time laid a foundation for a theory that transcended these narrow mercantilist goals.

# FOUR

# The
# *Second Treatise of Government*
# and the Foundation of
# Economic Society

THE EMPHASIS in this book so far has been on the contributions of Locke the practical economist who, writing on behalf of a policy measure that he advocated, happened to describe a set of economic principles which were important in furthering the development of economic science—a result which came about because of his ingrained habit of speculation upon the foundations of any problem with which he was dealing. If Locke had done no more than this for economics, he would have left a valuable legacy to his eighteenth- and nineteenth-century heirs in the form of a more structured science of economic behavior. But Locke also contributed to the progression of economic thought as a political philosopher; in the course of attempting to explore the legitimate basis of civil society, he managed to provide a philosophical basis for the legitimacy of economic society as well.

It is fitting that Locke should have described the philosophical foundations of economic activity in his major work on political philosophy, the *Second Treatise of Government*. It was this work, along with the *First Treatise* refuting Filmer's divine right of kings argument, which Locke wrote to justify the revolution against Charles II that Shaftesbury was plotting in 1679–80. The *Second Treatise* had to be devoted to establishing the morality of forcibly changing rulers under extreme circumstances, which meant that it had to establish a higher authority than the civil ruler to legitimize such action. This authority Locke found in a theory of natural law which implied a corresponding theory of natural rights of individuals apart from the rights guaranteed to them as citizens. Locke maintained that natural law dictated that the ultimate source of political sovereignty was with the individual, and a state could come into existence only when a group of sovereign individuals agreed to enter into a contract to relinquish some of their individual rights to a common ruler. In return, the ruler had to agree to protect their interests or suffer the consequences of his failure to uphold his part of the contract —removal from office and replacement with a more congenial ruler. In this way, by implying that Charles II had indeed failed in his primary duties to his subjects, Locke was able to lay the philosophical basis for the impending revolution. Although this is a political argument in a political treatise, it has a direct bearing on the present study. The major purpose of the *Second Treatise* was to establish that a revolution may take place when the ruler fails to do that which he has contracted to do: protect the best interests of his subjects. Its value here begins when Locke, in order to define exactly wherein those best interests lie, explains the origin and purpose of political society, because then it becomes evident that he is basing political society to a large extent on an economic foundation.

Locke believed that economic activity was present from the beginning of time and is the first and most important of human endeavors. It is the means by which men are able to survive in the world, and just as they have a right to survive, so they have a right to engage in economic activity and to enjoy the fruits thereof. Furthermore, economic activity led to the first kind of social interaction between individual men, and ultimately to the formation of civil society, whose purpose was that of protecting the economic society which was already in existence. Thus the first duty of the ruler is to protect and preserve the private property of the citizens under his rule. Locke does not begin with his conclusions, however, and in order to understand how he arrives at them, we must first turn to the analytic, if not the actual, starting point of his *Second Treatise,* the Lockean state of nature. It is here that he explains how men's natural rights guarantee both their right to the fruits of their economic labors and their right to form and dissolve governments as well.

The construct of a state of nature was a familiar feature of seventeenth- and eighteenth-century social thought. For Locke, a state of nature is defined by the fact there there is no agreed-upon civil authority governing the actions of men. While Locke treated the state of nature as a historical reality which could be found even in his time existing in the wilds of America, its main function in his thought is as an analytic device to reveal the essence of government by showing an existence without government.[1] Thus he claimed that in the absence of a civil government, all men are free and equal in the sense that no one individual has any natural right to rule any other; each man is the equal of every other in terms of legitimate political power. The reason that absolute individual sovereignty does not lead to complete chaos, Locke believes, is that each man has the law of nature to guide his actions. Although Locke is never explicit as to the content of this law of nature (either here or in his other writings), he does claim that its source is God, and that it is made known to men through their reason, if only they would choose to employ their intellects to that purpose.[2] What it teaches is that "no one ought to harm another in his life, health, liberty, or possessions."[3] In fact, since men are all "the workmanship of one omnipotent and infinitely wise Maker," and in the world to do His business, each person has a duty to preserve himself, and in addition, "when his own preservation comes not in competition," to do the best he can to "preserve the rest of Mankind."[4] Thus man has a natural

79

right to his life free from harm by other men, and two correlative duties: not to harm overtly another human, and to protect his own and other men's lives when the two are not in conflict. Since any impairment of one's liberty also threatens one's life, no man has a right to try to restrain any person's natural liberty, which also implies that a man has a right to protect himself from any attempted impairment. And finally, the right to life also implies a right to have possessions and therefore indicates that no one may rightfully harm any person in his possessions. How the right to own property derives from one's right to life, one of the most interesting features of Locke's state of nature, will be taken up shortly.

The law of nature, then, guarantees that Locke's state of nature will not be the "war of all against all" which characterizes that of Hobbes. This does not mean, however, that Locke therefore believed the state of nature would be a golden age of peace and tranquility. He notes, for example, that since in the state of nature each man would be his own judge and executor of the law, there would be a great temptation for men to be prejudiced in their own favor.[5] He also describes men as being, for the most part, "no strict observers of equity and justice," which causes life in the state of nature to be "very unsafe, very unsecure."[6] In fact, Locke was ambiguous as to the level of disorder one might expect to find in the state of nature, and this ambiguity has been a source of controversy among political philosophers. Much of Locke's ambiguity is removed, however, once one realizes that he does not describe the same amount of dissention as existing at all times in the state of nature. Rather, the degree of discord in the state of nature seems to be directly related to the degree of economic development that has taken place during this prepolitical time.

The remarkable feature of Locke's state of nature, which makes it especially interesting to economists, is his assumption that a wide variety of economic activities will take place prior to the existence of government. Instead of describing it as a Garden of Eden where men do not have to work for their daily bread, or alternatively, as a primitive state where men struggle along at a level of bare subsistence, Locke separated his definition of a state of nature from any required set of economic characteristics. In Locke's state of nature, people work, gather food, sow and reap, hire servants, create and use tools, exchange the products of their labor with one another and, eventually, use money. Not only do all these activities take place, but they lead to economic growth and the development of economic institutions which finally become incompatible with the continuation of a state of nature. When this occurs, men turn to forming a civil government to help maintain the economic development which has taken place. Specifically, property is created in the state of nature; it is the need to protect accumulated property that leads to the beginning of civil society. How this comes about is shown by Locke's theory of property.

The premise of Locke's famous theory of property is that God commanded men to survive and gave to all men in common the earth and its fruit to help them achieve this purpose.[7] To use any of the earth's resources, however, meant to take them away from someone else's potential use, and it was Locke's problem, and the problem of seventeenth-century political philosophers in general, to explain how these appropriated resources could become private property, legitimately excluding the claims of other men. Grotius and Pufendorf had both argued that private property was established in the state of nature by the consent of all mankind who once shared in the original communist ownership of these resources.[8] But since property existed only by the consent of society, such a theory implied that this consent could be withdrawn or modified by the society which had originally sanctioned it and an individual's property confiscated, a conclusion which Locke sought to avoid. Instead, he argued that private property was established in the state of nature not by the consent of mankind, but by natural law. Natural law dictated both that all men had common access to God's earthly resources, and that each man by virtue of his political equality with every other man owned his own person. This self-ownership, combined with man's right and duty to survive, permitted him to create property where none previously existed.

Locke's theory of property, then, rests on two basic assumptions: man has a right to maintain his life; and God has provided him with the means to do so. The entire world, according to Locke, is a vast pool of resources which God has given to all men in common to maintain themselves.[9] These common resources are only the raw materials of life which must be rendered useful to men through the medium of labor. Since a man's labor is also part of himself, as soon as he mixes his labor with a portion of the common pool of resources, he creates something new which is also a part of himself and so can belong to no other man. He creates valuable property, and since he creates it, he alone has a right to own it: "It being by him removed from the common state Nature placed it in, it hath by his labour something annexed to it, that excludes the common right of other Men. For this labour being the unquestionable property of the labourer, no man but he can have a right to what that is once joyned to, at least where there is enough, and as good left in common for others."[10]

Thus it is labor, a purposeful act, which establishes one's right to own property, rather than the consent of one's fellow man, but it is labor very broadly defined. That is, the labor which bestows property rights in Locke's opinion is of several distinct kinds. The first kind of labor which entitles a man to own property is also the most obvious: it is the kind that results from "the labour of his body, and the work of his hands,"[11] which includes any voluntary action on his part directed at sustaining himself. It may require some skill, as in the case of an Indian who kills a deer that is originally part of the common stock,[12] or it may require nothing more complex than motor action and intent, as is illustrated by a man gathering acorns to eat.[13] In both cases, as soon as a portion of the common stock is appropriated, it becomes lawful property resulting from a combination of man's labor and nature's gifts. This kind of labor is direct and unassisted human effort, needing the assistance only of nature to produce a product, and as such can be called proprietary labor. Contrary to the contentions of some commentators on Locke's political thought, however, this is not the only kind of labor Locke describes.[14] In addition, he defines "the grass my horse has bit; the turfs my servant has cut; and the ore I have digg'd"[15] as equivalent kinds of labor, all entitling the owner of the labor to property in the final product. Clearly, then, one's labor can also include the product of the effort of someone one has hired, the wage serving as a proxy for acquiring title to the result. Already there is implied a two-part division under the general category of labor, the employer and the employee, the one who directs the operation and the one who follows directions. In addition, Locke has a third category which he includes under the name of labor, which is already implied in the "grass my horse has bit." Insofar as the horse is an instrument of production, it constitutes capital, and the product of its services belongs to its owner.

While one can easily understand how Locke could conclude that the resources appropriated by a man's horse belonged to the owner of the horse, it might seem less understandable that Locke should argue that the product of a servant's labor should belong to the employer. Locke's reason for arguing this way, however, is explained by his view of the relationship between servants and employers. He claimed that a servant is originally a free agent who chooses to make a contract with his employer to do as his employer wishes (insofar as his employer does not ask him to do anything immoral), in return for a stated wage. What he subsequently does, then, is at his employer's direction and is a result of his employer's initiative, and since he has voluntarily agreed to trade a title to property for a sure wage, he is in no way harmed or exploited. Locke describes the relationship very precisely: "for a Free-man makes himself a servant to another, by selling him for a certain time, the service he undertakes to do, in exchange for wages he is to receive: and though this commonly puts him into the family of his Master, and under the ordinary discipline thereof; yet it gives the Master but a temporary power over him, and no greater, than what is contained in the contract between 'em."[16] The servant, far from being a slave or an object of exploitation, is to Locke's mind a free agent who makes a voluntary contract with an employer for a specific job, for a specific wage, and for a specific length of time. This relationship of servant to master can and has existed from the earliest times in the state of nature, and although Locke does not give a specific reason why a freeman would want to sell his labor to someone else when he could work for himself and acquire his own property, presumably Locke believed that a man would do it only if it were to his advantage. Locke indicates that not all men are of the same capabilities, and so he might have believed that a less capable man might prefer to work for a very able man rather than muddle along on his own, or, given the practice of English society of his time, he might have looked upon hired labor as characteristic of the very young and unskillful who were actually serving a kind of apprenticeship before setting out to earn their own property.[17]

Labor, then, means any human effort, and can consist of proprietary labor, hired labor, or the "labor" of capital or intermediate goods. The property created by any of these forms of labor belongs to the owner or, perhaps more accurately, to the entrepreneur who directed the factors of production to produce the property for him.

After having established an individual's right to own property in the state of nature, Locke goes on to define the right to property broadly enough to include both "the fruits of the earth and the earth itself,"[18] i.e., both the goods one creates and the land one cultivates. Furthermore, perhaps to justify this "strange doctrine" to his readers, that "the property of labour should be able to over-balance the community of land,"[19] Locke goes on to claim that the right to private property worked to the advantage of the population as a whole. The traditional justification of private property had been the Aristotelian one that men would take better care of what they owned, and the medieval Schoolmen had seen private property as symptomatic of the fallen state: it was a compromise with complete virtue that was necessary in the world in which we find ourselves. Locke directly challenged that view by making property a right in the state of nature, and continued by arguing that private property was beneficial to mankind because it derived from labor, and labor was productive.

Locke's accounts of the productivity of labor are no doubt familiar to most readers, since they have frequently been noted in history of thought textbooks, and have on occasion been used to support the erroneous notion that Locke had a labor theory of value in an economic sense.[20] Locke argued that private property was not only moral, but useful, because " 'tis labour indeed that puts the difference of value on every thing; and let any one consider, what the difference is between an acre of land planted with tobacco, or sugar, sown with wheat or barley; and an acre of the same land lying in common, without husbandry upon it, and he will find, that the improvement of labour makes the far greater part of the value."[21] The implication is that unassisted nature really provides very little that is useful to mankind. In fact, Locke gives a rough estimate of the relative importance of labor and land to the creation of goods valued by men: "I think it will be but a very modest computation to say, that of the products of the earth useful to the life of man 9/10 are the effects of labour: nay, if we will rightly estimate things as they come to our use, and cast up the several expenses about them, what in them is purely owning to nature, and what to labour, we shall find, that in most of them $99/_{100}$ are wholly to be put on the account of labour.''[22] This passage raises some interesting questions for the historian of economic thought. While it is clear here that Locke was illustrating the importance of labor to the creation of value, one wonders if perhaps he was also trying to indicate some quantitative measure of labor's contribution to production. Perhaps Locke was trying to measure the value of labor.

The key to understanding Locke's intention in the above and other such passages is in the phrase ''labor puts the difference of value'' on all things. That is, land lying fallow will produce a certain amount of grain growing wild without the assistance of labor, but cultivation will vastly increase both the quantity and quality of output. These increases in output are the actual measure of the increased value of land attributable to labor.

> For whatever Bread is more worth than Acorns, Wine than Water, and Cloth or Silk than Leaves, skins, or moss, that is wholly owing to labour and industry. The one of these being the food and raymant which unassisted nature furnishes us with; the other provisions which our industry and pains prepare for us, which how much they exceed the other in value, when anyone hath computed, he will then see, how much labour makes the far greatest part of the value of things, we enjoy in this world.[23]

Here he is referring to intrinsic value, the value of anything in sustaining human life, which is increased by ''human industry,''[24] but later on, when he wishes to be exact and put numbers to the increased value of land, he switches to a measure of value in exchange.

Locke's means for measuring the contribution of labor is to compare the output of two equal particles of land, one cultivated and one uncultivated, and his frame of reference for making his calculations is always America, the archetypical pool of unimproved resources, where "a King of a large and fruitful territory. . .feeds, lodges, and is clad worse than a day labourer in England."[25] The calculations can be made by comparing an acre of land in America, which is essentially unimproved, and one of equal fertility in England:

> An acre of land that bears here twenty bushels of wheat, and another in America, which, with the same husbandry, would do the like, are, without doubt, of the same natural, intrinsick value. But yet the benefit mankind receives from the one, in a year, is worth 5£. and from the other possibly not worth a Penny, if all the profit an Indian received from it were to be valued, and sold here; at least, I may truly say, not $\frac{1}{1000}$.[26]

In other words, the value of labor's contribution to final output is measured by the additional revenue which one can get from selling the products of cultivated land over the uncultivated: the measure of the value of labor is the market price of the output labor creates. Furthermore, it is the market price in an advanced, vigorous market like England's which may imply that only such a market correctly determines value. Obviously, since Locke describes the value of labor as being determined by the market price, rather than showing price as being somehow determined by the quantity of labor which goes into a product, he was far from describing a labor theory of value in either a classical or a Marxian sense.[27] What one can see in Locke's attempt to measure the contribution of labor to final output is if anything a crude productivity theory.

It would not be wise to stretch this point too far, because Locke seems to have totally lacked the logical concept that is vital to marginal calculation: varying the amounts of a factor to observe the result on output. Locke's effort was an all-or-nothing calculation: either cultivated or uncultivated land, either unimproved or improved-upon resources. Nevertheless, he did try to separate the contributions of at least two factors of production to the value of output, a necessary prerequisite to the development of a marginal productivity analysis. His concluding that it is "labour makes the far greatest part of the value of things, we enjoy in this world"[28] is at least partly due to his defining labor as labor and capital. (Labor is also defined to contain the category of technological progress, or "invention and arts," as Locke put it.)[29] Although none of these observations is sufficient to justify a claim of any kind of conscious pioneering on Locke's part, his ideas may have been significant in influencing later economists on this point.

If it is debatable that Locke's analysis points forward in time to the contributions of the marginalists, there can be no question of the resemblances between Locke's work and that of his older contemporary, Sir William Petty. There are obvious parallels in their handling of the problem of the contribution of land and labor to value and, although Petty was probably the more skillful of the two, the reasons for the differences between his work and Locke's have to do more with intent than ability. While it is impossible to say for certain that Locke was influenced by Petty, he did possess all of Petty's major economic works, including the all-important *A Treatise of Taxes and Contributions,* which he acquired in 1667, in time for it to have had an effect on his writing.[30] In addition, even where no influence is possible owing to respective dates of publication, there are similarities that should be noted as representative of a common attitude. But before we launch into any comparison between Petty's work and Locke's, a word of warning is in order. Any comparison of Petty's economic ideas as found in the *Treatise of Taxes* or any of his other works with Locke's economic ideas as found in the *Second Treatise* is bound to be somewhat strained, owing to the different natures of the two works. Locke was making a case for private ownership based on the virtues of industry and labor, while Petty was writing consciously economic essays aimed at specific economic problems, and although there are implications in each man's work that bear upon that of the other, the difference in intent should not be lost sight of. Ideally, we should compare Locke's *Some Considerations* with Petty's work. But since it is in the *Second Treatise* that Locke's theme, if not his intent, most nearly approaches Petty's, we must be satisfied with gleaning what we can from this imperfect comparison.

It is to be remembered first of all that Petty differed from Locke in his identification of the source of value. While Locke was convinced that "labour puts the difference of value on everything,"[31] Petty considered "that labour is the father and active principle of wealth, as lands are the mother,"[32] or that land and labor were mutually responsible for the creation of value. This is not to say that Locke denied the value of land altogether; indeed, he believed that a benevolent God provided man with all he needs to live well. But he also believed that natural resources were no more than potential wealth that could be actualized only by the labor of a human being. Given Locke's definition of labor as any kind of appropriation of the common stock (including so much as picking up an acorn from the ground), this conclusion is inescapable. It is not surprising, then, given their different attitudes toward the origin of wealth, that Petty and Locke should have different means of calculating the value of output. Locke believed that all value was the result of labor and so tried to estimate the contribution of labor to the value of the stock of wealth, while Petty, following his own definitions, attempted to find some means of evaluating the contribution of both land and labor to the value of final output. His method, found in the *Political Anatomy of Ireland,* was to allow a weaned calf to graze for one year on two acres of enclosed pastureland and then to measure the increase in the cow's weight. This increase, which Petty estimated would be about a hundred pounds or fifty days' food for one person, was the value (or rent) of the land. He went on: "But if a man's labour—for a year can make the said land to yield more than sixty [*sic*] days food of the same, or of any kind, then the over plus of days food is the wages of the man."[33] Here we see a more sophisticated attempt to determine factor value than Locke's, even though the procedure was the same: measuring output with and without the use of a factor of production. Locke's assertion that land is worth "scarce anything" is a mere tautology, nothing more than the necessary logical consequence of his definition of labor to include every attempt, no matter how slight, to satisfy bodily needs with the "gifts" of nature. Of course we see that Locke did not actually stick that close to his original definition and did allow unimproved land to have some value in Petty's sense, even if it was limited to $\frac{1}{10}$, $\frac{1}{100}$, or $\frac{1}{1000}$ part of all value.[34] Perhaps if Locke had addressed himself to the problem of measuring the contribution of factors of production in the context of an economic treatise, he would have come closer to Petty's analysis. In his economic works, however, he dismissed as irrelevant the determination of any kind of "natural value" aside from market price and turned his attention solely to the determination of market price, which was shown to be a result of supply and demand alone, with very little account taken of the phenomena surrounding them.

To summarize Locke's argument so far, he claims that labor is productive, creating goods of much greater value to consumers than does nature alone, and therefore it is only just that it should also create a title to property.

While private property may be a just institution, it may nevertheless lead to undesirable consequences if it is possible for some people to use up all the common resources in creating their own property, thereby leaving others with no way to support themselves. Locke denies that this is possible, however, because of the natural law limitation to the amount of property one can legitimately own in the state of nature. He has already given us a clue that there is such a limit: "labor being the unquestionable property of the laborer, no man but he can have a right to what that is once joined to, at least where there is enough and as good left in common for others." That "enough and as good" will in fact be left for others is guaranteed by God: "As much as any one can make use of to any advantage of life before it spoils; so much he may by his labour fix a property in. Whatever is beyond this, is more than his share, and belongs to others. Nothing was made by God for man to spoil or destroy."[35] An interesting feature of Locke's work is illustrated here. He often begins by stating a moral principle derived from God's authority which is not open to dispute, and then goes on to show how this principle is consistent with man's nature, or how nature provides the proper incentives for men to comply with this moral principle. In this case, having stated the proposition that men should not let resources spoil or go to waste because God forbids it, he now shows that in the state of nature (a) there was no incentive for men to try to gather more than they could use and so no incentive to waste resources, and (b) even if they did, it wouldn't make much difference anyway to the population as a whole:

> And thus considering the plenty of natural provisions there was a long time in the world, and the few spenders, and to how small a part of that provision the industry of one man could extend it self, and ingross it to the prejudice of others; especially keeping within the bounds, set by reason of what might serve for his use; there could be then little room for quarrels or contentions about property so established.[36]

That is, the state of nature as Locke has described it so far is one that is characterized by no resource scarcity. Populations are small and the world is large and abundantly supplied. One man's use of resources does not limit the effective amount available for others to use ("For he that leaves as much as another can make use of, does as good as take nothing at all'').[37] In addition, Locke imagined that in this early state of nature people would be nomadic, and hence there would be little ownership of land itself and even less possibility that one man's property might exclude another man's opportunity.[38] In such a setting, furthermore, there is virtually no incentive for any man to try to accumulate more property than he can make use of, presumably because there is no uncertainty about future provisions and because all of the goods he can acquire are perishable anyway.[39]

Even more interesting than the idea that lack of scarcity removes the incentive to accumulate property is his estimation of the social consequences of this fact of nature: ''there could be then little room for quarrels and contentions about property so established.''[40] Where men were nomadic, if a dispute did arise, it was easy just to move away from the source of contention. Thus at this stage in the state of nature, property disputes where each party had some legitimate claim would be unknown, leaving only the unjust claims of the ''quarrelsome and contentious'' for the adjudication of natural law. Clearly, even though men would be judges of their own disputes, right and wrong would be easily determined and the potential for discord in this state would be limited.

This kind of peaceful existence cannot continue, however, as populations grow and economic development takes place. Population growth, beginning to put pressure on the availability of resources, leads to eventual economic scarcity, while economic development leads to property accumulation by the more industrious individuals in the population, unequal distributions of wealth, and an increased potential for property disputes and criminal behavior.

The key to economic development in Locke's system is the beginning of the use of money. Although nature puts both a moral and an effective limit on the amount of property anyone can accumulate, this limit is not related to quantity, but to the consequences of accumulation. As long as nothing spoils, it doesn't matter how much actual property anyone owns. Consequently, Locke reasons, men will try to find ways of storing their excess products in some acceptable way, that is, by trading perishable goods for more durable ones that can be used in the future. In the course of this trading process, some one commodity, the most durable and easily tradable one, eventually becomes commonly acceptable as a money commodity. Locke describes this process as men consenting to use money.[41] While this is a rather strange use of the word *consent,* which we usually take to mean a formal contract, all Locke was trying to imply was that money came about voluntarily, as men tried to overcome a limitation nature placed on their economic activity. *Consent* not only implies a voluntary act, but also indicates that money is not a "natural" institution, that is, not deducible from natural law, but rather a man-made institution in keeping with natural law.[42] This use of consent it consistent with his more formal contract theory of government, where government is also a man-made institution and where the contract (explicit in this case) is entered into to avoid difficulties in the state of nature. The conditions of existence are "natural," that is, every man must survive, and he must eat and clothe and house himself to do so. Every man has as much right to perform these tasks as every other man, and if men use their intelligence to find better ways to perform them, such "man-made" adaptations are consistent with nature as long as they do not violate the few obvious precepts of natural law. Thus the agreement to use money enables men to get around the consequences of the natural limit to property ownership (no accumulation of property), because it does not violate the natural limit of the amount one can use without spoiling or waste; the use of money is therefore completely within the bounds of just or moral behavior.[43]

While the use of money is a reasonable way of getting around the difficulties of storing wealth, its consequences are profound. It permits the "more industrious and rational," and therefore the more productive, to accumulate the products of their labor and thus to increase their wealth relative to the less industrious or talented.[44] This leads inevitably to envy, and envy leads inevitably to more property disputes and common thievery. The abilities of individuals to be the judges in their own disputes become severely taxed. It becomes more and more likely that they will want to delegate their policing and judicial powers to another institution to improve their security and release them from a relatively nonproductive responsibility. Government is the answer to this desire.[45]

It must be pointed out, however, that while the unequal distribution of wealth does increase the probability of dissention in the state of nature, it is not the sufficient condition for the institution of a government. The ultimate cause is scarcity of land brought about both by ownership of private property and by increasing populations.[46] Even if wealth is relatively evenly distributed, there would still be problems as increasing populations put pressure on common resources which are growing ever more limited in supply. Even if every property-owner has only as much property as he needs to support his household, if the common resources are no longer free goods, property disputes and complaints where right and wrong are not easily distinguishable are inevitable. Government then necessarily must take on the task of regulating property as well as of protecting it.

To summarize the argument so far: in the state of nature each man is the political equal of every other man. Its conditions of existence are such that men must labor to survive, and this labor, consisting of mixing their own persons with God-given common resources, creates property. Originally, populations were small relative to resources, and that fact, coupled with the natural law limit to property ownership, ensured that each man would have as many resources at his disposal as he needed for survival. Some men are more industrious than others, however, and produce more than they need immediately. These have an incentive to try to find ways to store their excess, which leads to bartering of perishables for durables until a money commodity is established. Money permits unequal accumulation of wealth as well as increased economic activity which, coupled with increasing popula- tions, leads to a scarcity of land, increasing dissention, and more frequent legitimate disputes. Existence in the state of nature without a supreme governing body, becomes very costly, and hence men have an incentive to form civil society to set up a government both to protect and to regulate their property.

So far I have described the motivation for the social con- tract as being strictly the protection of physical property. This is in fact what Locke describes in his chapter "On Property." Later in the treatise, however, he broadens the basis for men's desire for government and implies a much less orderly state of nature than the property chapter would have us envision:

> If man in the state of nature be so free, as has been said; If he be absolute lord of his own person and possessions, equal to the greatest, and subject to no body, why will he part with his Freedom? . . . To which 'tis obvious to answer, that though in the state of nature he hath such a right, yet the enjoyment of it is very uncertain, and constantly exposed to the invasion of others. For all being kings as much as he, every man his equal, and the greater part no strict observers of equity and justice, the enjoyment of the property he has in this state is very unsafe, very unsecure. This makes him willing to quit a condition, which however free, is full of fears and continual dangers: And 'tis not without reason, that he seeks out and is willing to join in society with others who are already united, or have a mind to unite for the mutual preservation of their lives, liberties and estates, which I call by the general name, property.[47]

In the above passage, it is not just some individuals who will invade the property rights of others, but the majority, men being for the most part "no strict observers of equity and justice." Obviously Locke believes that natural law is sufficient to define individual rights in the state of nature, including the rights to life, liberty, and estate, but since men generally do not interpret natural law in an unbiased manner, natural law is not sufficient to guarantee that an individual can enjoy his rights. Notice that in the above passage, Locke has defined property to include life, liberty, and estate. This was a common usage of the seventeenth century: people were thought to have property rights in their persons (Locke has already used this idea in his theory of property) and in their political and religious freedom.[48] Although the term *rights* is a moral term, it would not be contrary to Locke's intent to describe these properties not simply as rights, but also as attributes descriptive of human existence. Human existence in the state of nature presupposes life, liberty in the sense of natural political equality, and estate in the form of goods used for consumption. It is to maintain and protect these "properties," threatened in the state of nature, that people resort to governments. Yet to form governments, men must give up their "equality, liberty and executive power," which means trading off some of their freedom of action for more security in their lives and estates. They will do this, Locke claims, only if the government will make them better off than they were in the state of nature.[49] Specifically, government must be less costly to them than the state of nature if the government is to be a preferred alternative.

The *Second Treatise,* then, states the principle which relates the economy to the political realm. Economic activity is primary because it exists in the state of nature: it is the activity by which men fulfill God's charge to survive, and it develops spontaneously and in accordance with natural law. Government is a man-made institution in that it does not develop spontaneously but requires a conscious agreement on the part of all individuals to obtain legitimacy. Once it obtains legitimacy through consent, however, it, rather than the individual, becomes the interpreter of natural law which it embodies in the civil law. Because government is a man-made institution created for a specific purpose, it can never act contrary to that purpose, the protection of property broadly defined as life, liberty, and estate. The enjoyment of all three of these properties depends upon social order, and it is to ensure this order that men voluntarily subject themselves to a common rule of law. By defining property as he does, Locke is implying that the government's charge to protect estate is no less important than its charge to protect life and liberty. In this sense, then, the government as an institution is subordinate to the requirements of economic activity.

While the government is formed originally to protect the private property created by individuals in the state of nature, once the social contract is entered into, the government has the right and duty to regulate property for the common good. Yet neither the government's right nor its power to regulate property is unbounded. There are important limits to the government's ability to regulate property that are best understood by more closely examining the nature of the original contract to form civil society.

The original contract is "that which makes the community, and brings men out of the loose state of nature, into one political society...the agreement which everyone has with the rest to incorporate and act as one body, and so by distinct Commonwealth."[50] No man can withdraw his consent to be a member of civil society once he has given it.[51] The commonwealth therefore can never be dissolved from within by mutual agreement, but can revert to the state of nature only in the case of foreign conquest.[52] This commonwealth has the power given it by its members to legislate laws and punish transgressors and to regulate the property of its citizens.[53] Since the establishment of laws to protect property was the purpose for organizing into society, Locke believed that society had to have the right to regulate the property it was supposed to protect. Anyone living in the society who had not given explicit consent to its formation was not considered to be a full member and therefore could withdraw from it whenever he chose, but as long as he remained in it he was presumed to have given tacit consent to its authority and therefore was expected to behave according to its laws. When and if he wished to withdraw, he was required to give up all his land, under the assumption that only the benefits of society had allowed him to enjoy it in the first place and therefore he had no right to remove it from society.[54] What started out as a collection of individuals banding together for their mutual benefit thus seems to turn into a body politic with an importance beyond that of any one of its members and with the perpetuation of itself as its aim.

Willmoore Kendall contended over the years that Locke's failure to enunciate specific limitations to the powers of society in this respect makes him far more a majority-rule democrat than the advocate of limited government that he is claimed to be.[55] Specifically, Kendall's argument is that in Lockean society, property is regulated for the public good by the will of the majority, with virtually no limit to its power to alienate the so-called inalienable right men have to their property. In fact, Kendall maintains that even in Locke's state of nature, the right to property is explained as a contribution to the public good rather than as a right that need not be defended, and the burden of proof is always upon the property-owner to prove that his property will not cause others to suffer as a result of his ownership. Kendall claims that "where Locke has to choose between the individual's right of property in that which he has mixed his labor and the common right of men to their preservation, he unhesitatingly sacrifices the former to the latter."[56]

Kendall's argument, while persuasive, can be countered on several points. First, Locke does not defend property in the state of nature as a contribution to the public good: this is a fringe benefit of property ownership. In civil society the conditions change because, given the undependable morality of men, great property can exist only with the aid of society, and therefore society's welfare should be looked after first and foremost. When Locke defines wherein that welfare consists, however, as he does in *Some Considerations,* it turns out that the property-owners rank very high on his list of those people who should not be allowed to suffer.[57] Even more emphatically, he argues that it is precisely when the government fails to protect the property-owner to the extent that he is no better off with government than without that revolutions are justified. Furthermore, whereas Locke does give a great deal of latitude to society in its power over the individual, this latitude is strictly circumscribed when it comes to the powers of government, which are given by a separate contract.

The commonwealth, or society, and the government are two distinct concepts to Locke, and the contract to form a commonwealth did not necessarily imply a contract to form any particular kind of government. *The government* refers to a specific ruling body composed ideally of a legislative, executive, and federative power vested in at least two different groups.[58] Any particular ruling body was allowed by society to maintain power only as long as it acted for the benefit of the people. Since the people were united to protect their property, "whenever the legislators endeavor to take away, and destroy the property of the people, or reduce them to slavery under arbitrary power, they put themselves in a state of war with the people, who are thereupon absolved from any further obedience, and are left to the common refuge, which God hath provided for all men, against force and violence."[59] In such circumstances, "it [the power originally given to government] devolves to the people, who have a right to resume their original liberty, and, by the establishment of a new legislature (such as they shall think fit) provide for their own safety and security, which is the end for which they are in society."[60] While the contract to form society is indissoluble except through foreign conquest, governments can and should be dissolved when they fail in their primary task, the protection of private property.

Although Locke thus fulfills his major aim in writing the *Second Treatise,* which was to give society the right to change its governors, he is careful not to allow this to imply a collapse of society as well. The commonwealth remains intact, ready to pass on all its rules and powers to the new government once it is duly chosen by consent of the people.[61] To a man who is trying to provide a philosophical basis for an impending revolution, one can see the obvious advantages this theory has over one that allows men to return to a state of nature after the government falls. In principle it allows the economic structure among individuals to remain intact throughout the political upheaval: governments may rise and fall, but the leaders of a society remain the leaders in spite of all, and the economy continues to function as before. There could be no question of a revolution that involves a land redistribution, because land can never again revert to the common state. Once it has been converted into property through labor, it can only be regulated, never expropriated from its owner; and if regulation of property implies a limitation of property rights, Locke's intention, nevertheless, was to protect that property and those rights from an even more limiting factor, the whims of royalty which he believed had been encroaching upon the safety of private property and disrupting the economy.

Locke's motives for setting up such a theory of the origin and purpose of society have been analyzed by scores of political scientists and philosophers. Besides Kendall, the most interesting for our purposes is C. B. MacPherson, who has built a case for Locke's being the archdefender of unlimited capitalist appropriation.[62] In defending his opinion of Locke as the original apologist for capitalism, MacPherson puts forth some convincing and original arguments. Since many of his conclusions are colored by Marxian preconceptions about the morality of capitalism, however, they should be held up to critical analysis.

To MacPherson Locke's major achievement is that he set up natural law limits to the amount of property any one person may lawfully own and then found a loophole to allow men to circumvent those limits.[63] He arrives at his conclusion by much the same route followed here, starting with the conditions under which property is created in the state of nature and then examining the transition occasioned by the introduction of money. He correctly identifies the steps Locke takes in arriving at the beginning of civil society and makes the crucial observation that Locke presents the economy as independent of the political structure. Although much of MacPherson's analysis of Locke's system is identical to the analysis presented here, in the interpretation of that system MacPherson and I differ greatly.

MacPherson identifies two important potential limitations to the amount of property anyone can own in Locke's state of nature, each of which is overcome in some way or another by the invention of money.[64] The most important is the "spoilage" limitation ("as much as anyone can make use of to any advantage of life before it spoils; so much he may by his labor fix a property in"),[65] which money overcomes by providing a nonperishable means for men to store their excess wealth. The problem with this part of Locke's account, according to MacPherson, is that Locke never provides an adequate reason in the *Second Treatise* for men to desire to own more than they can use for the conveniences of life. He believes he finds Locke's reason in *Some Considerations:* men desire excess wealth so they can employ land and money as capital for the increase of trade. MacPherson argues that Locke was a mercantilist who was interested in the accumulation of capital for its own sake in order to enrich the nation.[66] This interpretation, although interesting, is inaccurate in several respects. First of all, it makes the same mistake Locke has been accused of making, that of identifying money and capital. As we saw in chapter 3, Locke recognized very clearly that money was valuable only insofar as it could be exchanged for goods and services, and the fact that it could yield a return to its owner was a result of the fact that it was valuable to a businessman who could make a return above the rate of interest he had to pay for its use. In other words, Locke clearly understood that capital was productive in the sense of creating value, and that money was only one form of capital, just as he regarded money capital as representing only one function of money. MacPherson, however, claims that its function as capital was the main function of money in Locke's thought. He offers no substantiation of this claim (and, indeed, he would be hard put to do so from the text of either *Some Considerations* or the *Two Treatises*). Second of all, MacPherson makes the mistake of thinking that the only purpose of capital for Locke is to "beget further capital by profitable investment."[67] He quotes some notes on trade which Locke never published:

> The chief end of trade is riches and power which beget each other. Riches consists in plenty of moveables, that will yield a price to foraigners, and are not like to be consumed at home, but especially in plenty of gold and silver. Power consists in numbers of men, and ability to maintaine them. Trade conduces to both these by increasing your stock and your people. And they each other.[68]

These notes, to be found on an unattached sheet in the Bodleian Library, are headed "Trade, Essay 1674," and may represent some ideas which Locke was planning to incorporate into an essay at some future date. Most likely they did in fact become part of the foreign trade section of *Some Considerations,* which itself was the result of twenty-odd years of thoughts on the subject of economy.[69] It should be evident that these few notes cannot on their own be considered the key to Locke's thought to the exclusion of Locke's two major published essays on economics, yet this is exactly what

MacPherson is saying when he cites the "Trade" notes as support of his thesis that Locke was interested in the accumulation of capital for its own sake. If one does consult the works Locke chose to publish on the subject, one finds that Locke's ideas were far more sophisticated than MacPherson believes. There is no doubt that Locke understood that capital must be replaced if the standard of living of a nation is to be maintained, just as he knew that the only way for an individual or a society to grow rich in the good things of life was to increase its capital stock.[70] In this sense, Locke, like almost every other economist then and now, would be in favor of a constantly increasing capital stock, but this in no way suggests that he believed that capital or money should be accumulated for its own sake. The desire men have of accumulating more than they can use immediately is a very rational desire to improve their standard of living, or to increase the number of people that can be supported by a given geographical area.

MacPherson goes on to discuss the "sufficiency" limit to property, the stipulation that there will always be "enough and as good" left over for anyone else when a man creates private property. He correctly points out that this limitation is not a direct tenet of natural law, but is instead a consequence of the first ("spoilage") limitation, and that although both limitations disappear when money is invented, permitting men to accumulate real property, especially land, no one will suffer as a result of a land shortage since it will always be possible to make a living some way. Thus he claims that Locke substitutes "sufficiency in making a living" for "sufficiency in land" so that as long as no one is prevented from supporting himself, there is no cause for anyone to complain about the nonuniversal ownership of land.[71] This excellent insight into Locke's theory points out the actual benefits that Locke believed to result from the ownership of private property and the use of money. If MacPherson had only gone one step farther and pointed out that once money becomes a proxy for accumulated wealth, the total stock of wealth that can be owned by members of a community is no longer limited by the amount of land to which it has access,[72] but actually increases, he would have understood Locke's intentions completely.

What MacPherson argues is that even though Locke allows for the entire value of the common stock to increase as a result of private ownership, he makes no provision for the equitable distribution of this increased value, which MacPherson believes will accumulate in the hands of the landowners. He supports this contention by quoting section 37 of the *Second Treatise,* wherein Locke describes the value of private cultivation to mankind:

> To which let me add, that he who appropriates land to himself by his labour, does not lessen but increase the common stock of mankind. For the provisions serving to the support of humane life, produced by one acre of inclosed and cultivated land, are (to speak much within compasse) ten times more, than those, which are yeilded by an acre of land, of an equal richnesse lyeing wast in common. And therefor he, that incloses land and has a greater plenty of the conveniencys of life from ten acres, than he could have from an hundred left to nature, may truly be said, to give ninety acres to mankind. For his labour now supplys him with provisions out of ten acres, which were but the product of an hundred lying in common.[73]

MacPherson says that this analysis assumes "that the increase in the whole product will be distributed to the benefit, or at least not to the loss, of those left without enough land"[74] and thereby gives no assurance of equity in possessions. He fails to understand that what Locke is saying in this passage is that when labor is added to land, it produces more output than land would alone, so that if it took one hundred acres of land lying fallow to support one human life, and only ten acres of cultivated land to support that same human life, the other ninety acres have been freed to support other lives and so are "given to mankind." The common stock is increased not because more output can be gotten from the same amount of land, as MacPherson implies, although this is also true. The common stock is by definition that which is not any part of someone's property, and so it could not possibly be increased by an increased output on private land. The common stock is physically increased when a man cultivates his own ground because he then uses less of the common stock to support himself than he did when he was just an idle consumer. In this way, there is no need for him to distribute his output to improve the lot of mankind.

MacPherson's real argument lies not with this passage, but with the problem of the benefit to society when there is no more land left in common. He shows that Locke makes the assumption that the standard of living of everyone will increase regardless of who owns the property ("a king of a large and fruitful territory there feeds, lodges, and is clad worse than a day labourer in England"), first because land is more productive when it is cultivated, and second because men can hire themselves out as wage laborers to get a share of this increased productivity. We remember that Locke believed that economy was logically and temporally prior to government and described a complex economic structure existing in the state of nature including the use of wage labor and money exchange. MacPherson criticizes such a theory as "incredible,"[75] or "patently absurd,"[76] but nevertheless agrees that it fits Locke's assumptions about man which presumably are incredible and patent absurdities also. These assumptions are that men are rational enough to make contracts and rational enough to abide by them, assumptions MacPherson considers appropriate only if men are considered in the "abstract."[77] Evidently, according to MacPherson, in the concrete men are not rational enough to make and keep contracts without the existence of governments. However, MacPherson grants all of Locke's premises and then goes on to try to show that he was implying a class system wherein the laborer who is forced to "alienate" his labor in return for a wage and so undergo a "dehumanizing" process is an inferior member of society with only limited rational and political powers.[78]

To support his contention, MacPherson quotes a passage where Locke describes the mind-dulling effect of the kind of work most laborers must do, and several references where Locke mentions that laborers generally live at the subsistence level. However, in none of these passages is either of these effects portrayed as a necessary or even desirable consequence of capitalist activity. Locke did mention in several places that the workers usually live "from hand to mouth," but this was no iron law of wages but rather an observation of a general condition of the time. Moreover, when Locke says this in connection with his description of the velocity of money, he is referring not to any wretched conditions of English peasantry but to the fact that laborers usually have no other source of income than their labor and usually spend every penny they earn without saving anything. This says nothing about their standard of living, which will vary with the prosperity of the nation.[79]

And this brings us once again to the motive for Locke's writing. MacPherson calls Locke a mercantilist in his economics and an apologist for capitalist appropriation in his philosophy. But it has already been shown that there can be little justification for calling Locke's economics mercantilist, although he did agree with many mercantilist conclusions. About all he shared with the mercantilist outlook was a desire for a prosperous and healthy nation, a desire which was by no means peculiar to that group of economists. As for Locke's motives, if he wanted a strong and stable nation it was to support a large, wealthy, and prosperous population, and he believed that the only way to achieve his goal was through a well-functioning capitalist economy.[80] MacPherson says Locke was an apologist for capitalist appropriation, but if in the course of Locke's arguments he provides a justification for capitalism, it is only incidental to his major purpose of asserting the right of free men to provide for their own well-being to the best of their ability. If capitalism is justified, it is only because it is a consequence of men's asserting that right through their ownership of private property. To Locke private property is completely moral in that it grows from men's application of natural law, operates to reward industry and punish sloth, and has the effect of benefiting the entire commonwealth.

Whether or not economies could or did ever exist prior to the formation of government, Locke's real contribution is his assertion that the functioning of the economy is a primary force in holding civil society together. The economy is the major motivation behind the compact to form society in the first place, its protection justifies the powers of government, and its needs must come before those of royal pleasure, national pride, or foreign conquest. And since it is the ultimate source of the welfare of the community, the mismanagement of the economy and the loss of freedom this engendered could, and did, justify a revolution.

# FIVE

# John Locke, Social Scientist

WE HAVE ALREADY noted William Letwin's thesis that Locke was an early scientific economist. Letwin's argument was that Locke enunciated economic laws in an objective attempt to understand how the economy functioned rather than to justify his personal prejudices.[1] The next question is the related, but still different, problem of whether or not Locke can be considered an early social scientist. It is not customary to think of social science as existing in the seventeenth century: one usually associates the beginnings of social science with the eighteenth century and the work of David Hume or Adam Smith. Yet if social science means an attempt to explain the actions of human beings on the basis of assumptions about uniquely human characteristics, it is not unreasonable to expect to find early efforts at social science existing prior to the more conscious attempts of the eighteenth and nineteenth centuries. In fact, a good argument can be made that Locke's writings on politics and economics constitute one such early effort at social science.

A precedent exists for arguing that Locke was an early social scientist in Joseph Schumpeter's *History of Economic Analysis*.[2] There Schumpeter noted Locke's contributions to the seventeenth-century theory of natural law, and ranked Locke along with Hobbes, Grotius, and Pufendorf, among others, as philosophers who, despite their Protestantism, were in the Scholastic tradition. These philosophers, he claimed, "were of the same professional type as the scholastics. . .went about the same task, by the same method, in much the same spirit,"[3] and therefore could only be called laical or Protestant Scholastics. They were all influenced either directly or indirectly by medieval and late Scholastic writings, especially on natural law and jurisprudence, and in addition they followed much the same intellectual route the Scholastics had followed by going back to most of the same sources in ancient Greek and Roman literature. Most importantly, this group had as their aim according to Schumpeter the formulation of a comprehensive social science, "a comprehensive theory of society in all its aspects and activities—in which economics was neither a very important nor an independent element."[4]

Schumpeter's characterization of Locke as a Protestant Scholastic is appealing first of all because of its plausibility. We have already seen how Locke as a political philosopher based his theory of society on natural law, a concept which can be traced back through Scholastic literature to Roman and Greek origins. Further, we remember that although Locke was for a certain period of time a practising physician and closely associated with the "new science" of his century, he was also an Oxford don, a scholar in Greek and Roman literature, and a well-read gentleman familiar with all the intellectual currents of his day. His education had been solidly classical, even "Scholastic" (although not Catholic), and his travels in France, Belgium, Holland, and Germany introduced him to Continental writers who would be even more likely than he to be influenced by Scholastic ideas and methods. In his political philosophy, his debt to Grotius is well known,[5] and Grotius's debt to late Scholasticism has been documented on nearly every page of his writings.[6] There can be little doubt that Locke as a natural law philosopher absorbed many concepts typical of Scholastic thought and was a carrier of Scholastic tradition. While the connection between Scholasticism and Locke's economics is less well known, it can be shown that here, too, Locke's approach is much the same as that of the late Scholastics, and uses terms and concepts common to Aristotelian-Scholastic tradition. His distinction between value in use and value in exchange, his theory of money, his theory of price, and even his little-known discussion of the just price which will be discussed later in this chapter all serve to illustrate his links to Aristotelian and Scholastic economics.[7]

While it is doubtless true that Locke absorbed and passed on many Scholastic ideas in his political and economic writings, the more relevant problem for our discussion is to what degree Locke's writings fit Schumpeter's definition of the Scholastic task: a "comprehensive theory of society...in which economics was neither a very important nor an independent element." That he had accepted many Scholastic terms does not mean that Locke was creating a comprehensive social science in the Scholastic tradition. Apparently Schumpeter himself felt some reservations about ascribing such a motive to Locke because he claimed that although Locke's political theory fits the Scholastic method, his contributions to economics "stand in no relation to either his philosophy or his political theory."[8] If this is true, however, it contradicts Schumpeter's original description of Scholasticism. Surely, if one were trying to develop a comprehensive social science, one's political and economic theories would have to bear some relationship to each other, since both are concerned with major aspects of social life. While Schumpeter doubted that such a connection existed in Locke's work, it is our contention that Locke did have a "comprehensive theory of society" in both his economic and political writings. We have already hinted at this connection in the foregoing discussion of Locke's theory of the origin of political society. In chapter 4 it was argued that Locke's theory of the origin and purpose of government rested in large part on his understanding of the nature and consequences of economic activity. In addition it can be shown that Locke believed civil government to be naturally subordinate to the economy in its function in social life, and that the ability of the government to play an active role in the economy was therefore limited. Although Locke never purposely sat down to write a treatise on social science, his description of the role of government in economic life shows that he had a consistent view of society in his economic and political writings which was based on his perception of human nature and which presumed some kind of natural social order. Furthermore, Locke's theory of society was buttressed by a belief in the ultimate morality of the natural social order which he described.

The first argument for the intellectual connection between Locke's political and economic writings is circumstantial: they were both inspired by his connection with the first earl of Shaftesbury who encouraged Locke to communicate his thoughts on economic and political issues. Locke began writing *Some Considerations* in 1669 while a member of Shaftesbury's household and continued to revise it until its ultimate publication in 1692, two years after his return from Holland. He also wrote the *Second Treatise* while under Shaftesbury's influence, most likely in 1679–80, and it too was not published until Locke's return from exile. Both were carefully worked out pieces of reasoning on problems of social order despite the fact that the immediate purpose of one was to convince Parliament of the inappropriateness of a proposed bill, and of the other to provide an intellectual justification for revolution. It is therefore reasonable to expect that Locke would have had the same philosophy in mind during the composition of both works. The almost simultaneous publication of the two works, however, is but a minor argument in favor of the unity of thought between them. The real argument is in the content of the two essays. Although they were written for different purposes, they both deal with the problem of the limitations of government, one in the political realm, the other in the economic.

Locke's arguments for the limitations of government in the political realm are well known. In fact, his name is almost synonymous with the philosophy of political liberalism in the nineteenth-century sense. We have already explored the philosophical basis for Locke's theory of limited government in the preceding chapter, where we examined how Locke used his labor theory of property, a theory grounded in natural law, to explain the progress of civilization from a state of nature to civil society. He argued that government was formed by a contractual arrangement among a group of individuals for the specific purpose of protecting their rights to life, liberty, and estate, rights that were in jeopardy in the state of nature. Government was therefore naturally subordinate to that purpose, and as a result limited in its ability to control its citizens, who had the ultimate right to dispose of a government acting contrary to their interests.

Since Locke stressed the protection of physical property as the primary motivation for and purpose of government, it is pertinent to ask how he envisioned this role once civil society is established. Since government was formed in part to eliminate property disputes which arose in an economy characterized by scarcity of land, Locke argued that in the state of nature labor gave men the right to property, but "in governments the laws regulate the right of property, and the possession of land is determined by positive constitutions."[9] Unfortunately, Locke never specifies what kind of laws regarding property would be passed or how the constitution would determine the possession of land.

As we have already noted, Locke's statement that government can regulate the right to property can be interpreted to support Willmoore Kendall's majority rule view of Locke's political philosophy.[10] Even though men may still have the right to own property under civil government, if the specific kinds of property which they are entitled to enjoy are determined by the government and not natural law, then the test of having labored to produce a good may no longer be sufficient to legitimize ownership, because the government, operating within some constitutional framework, might be able to pass any laws regarding property ownership that had the support of the majority of the citizens. If this is indeed what Locke meant to say, then his natural rights defense of private property in the state of nature is worthless as a guide to property ownership in civil society, and the very result he wished to avoid with his labor theory of property, that is, that one owned property legitimately only with the consent of the rest of the population, is in fact the guiding principle of property ownership in a representative government. If this interpretation is correct, Locke's reputation as a defender of natural rights apart from government is highly overrated. The fact that Locke did not provide a guide to the specific kinds of property laws which government should enact should make us hesitate to accept the above argument, however. When one does search his writings for some guiding principle for property ownership in civil society, the only one to be found is that the purpose of government is to "preserve the property of all the members of that society, as far as is possible," without any indication of how far that is.[11]

Since the disorder engendered by property ownership in the state of nature was a major motivating factor in the origin of government, we can infer that the government must also maintain the order necessary for the enjoyment of property in civil society, but how much economic freedom is to be traded for order is a problem Locke does not confront directly in the *Second Treatise.* The only principle he clearly states is that property must not be less secure than it was in the state of nature, or there will be no incentive for individuals to support and obey the government.[12] The implication is that if civil laws do not conform at least roughly to natural laws, and if they are not applied equally to all citizens, individuals will replace the existing government with one more consistent with natural law. Thus natural law as interpreted by individual citizens acting in commonwealth is still the final source of political legitimacy. Furthermore, Locke argues that once civil laws regarding property are established, the government must obey those laws, and under no circumstances may it dispose of private property arbitrarily. It was after all the theme of the *Second Treatise* that when governments infringe too much on their citizens' enjoyment of their property, the citizens have a right to dispose of their government.

One wishes Locke had been more explicit in the *Second Treatise* about the role the government should take in regulating property, because the regulation of property rights is, by implication, also the regulation of economic activity. That is, the government might make specific assignments of property rights, which would have an indirect effect on the kinds of economic activities which citizens will undertake; or the government might control the economic activities directly in an attempt to alter the ownership of physical property. Thus the state's ability to regulate property rights can be interpreted as the ability to control economic behavior as well as the fruits of economic behavior. Therefore, if we knew what kind of power Locke believed the government should have over the regulation of property, we would begin to discover how great a role he believed it should play in the regulation of economic activity, and by implication get a clue to his beliefs regarding the behavior of the economic system.

Although the economic essays do not specifically discuss the philosophical problems involved in property regulation, they are more explicit about the role government should take in regulating economic activity than Locke's political work. This is to be expected, of course, since they were written to give advice on economic policy, and policy presupposes some idea of the proper role of government in the economy as well as some understanding of how the economy functions. What perhaps may be unexpected, however, is the degree to which the economic role of government as espoused in *Some Considerations* is consistent with Locke's theory of property in the state of nature described in the *Second Treatise.*

Since the subject of *Some Considerations* is economic policy, it is significant that Locke's major stress in this essay is on the limitations of the government's ability to legislate economic phenomena. The premise of his argument is that the economy operates according to certain laws, laws which he states as positively as if they were laws of the physical universe, the implication being that the government is powerless to alter them and hence cannot legislate contrary to them. Specifically, Locke argues that the government is incapable of regulating prices since prices are governed by "Laws of Value" that are beyond the control of civil laws.[13]

We have already analyzed Locke's arguments against one form of price regulation, setting a legal rate of interest below the "natural" rate: if the legislation is effective in preventing loans at other than the legal rate, the consequences will be a restriction of the supply of money and a disruption of trade because of increased uncertainty, while if the law is successfully circumvented, the results will be a higher market rate of interest, the elimination of riskier loans, and again the disruption of trade because of inconvenience and the increased cost of transacting loans. Although the consequences of regulating the rate of interest were his primary topic, Locke takes pains to compare the futility of interest regulation to the futility of any kind of price regulation. He claims that trying to maintain a below-market rate of interest is as useless as trying to control the price of wheat in a famine, and he argues in general that, "Experience will show, that the price of things will not be regulated by laws, though the endeavors after it will be sure to prejudice and inconvenience trade, and put your affairs out of order."[14]

While there is no question that Locke treated the laws of economics as if they were equivalent in importance to the laws of the physical universe (this is the point of Letwin's analysis of Locke), an equally important question that has not received attention in the literature is to what forces Locke attributed the operation of the laws of economics. Were they merely observed regularities that perhaps had no ultimate explanation, or did they rest on some even more abstract generalizations about human nature? It is only if the latter explanation is correct that we can consider Locke truly a social scientist in the sense of developing a science of human action based on observations of or assumptions about human beings.

The nature of Locke's economic essays makes the answer to this problem somewhat obscure, but the answer is nevertheless discernible to the careful reader. It can be inferred from Locke's writings that the reason that price regulation cannot work, the reason that attempts at such regulation invariably lead to consequences far different from and far more sinister than those intended by the regulators, is that human beings will always pursue their own economic self-interest. While it is nowhere stated thus precisely, the assumption of economic rationality is implicit in all of Locke's analysis of human action. For example, he recognizes that consumers with given tastes will respond to relative price changes by substituting cheaper goods for the more expensive goods which they had been accustomed to consuming.[15] Further, he argues that sellers will be responsive to potential profits in their decisions to supply products.[16] In both cases, he is assuming rational economic behavior. While this assumption is not new with Locke (Saint Augustine had described the desire to buy cheap and sell dear as one of the deepest of human desires, and the abstraction of economic man can be found in the writings of the late Scholastics),[17] Locke used this "fact" of human nature to show that any attempt to set prices at other than market-clearing levels will cause individual economic actors to find ways to subvert the laws in pursuit of their own self-interest:

it will be impossible, by any contrivance of law, to hinder men, skilled in the power they have over their own goods, and the ways of conveying them to others, to purchase money to be lent them at what rate soever their occasions shall make it necessary for them to have it. . . 'tis the want of money drives men to that trouble and charge of borrowing: and proportionably to this want, so will every one have it, whatever price it cost him. Wherein the skillful, I say, will always so manage it, as to avoid the prohibition of your law, and keep out of its penalty, do what you can.[18]

In other words, economic incentives are too powerful to be overcome by legislation.

If this sounds more like a description of the economics of Adam Smith than of John Locke, it is because Locke was in many respects Smith's anticipator. He was not trying to build a science of economic behavior based on human action so consciously as was Smith, but he was nevertheless trying to explain human behavior in a systematic way. This is true of his political philosophy where he tried to deduce civil society from natural law and human nature, and it is true of his economics where he stated laws of economics, laws of price determination in particular, which functioned because of human nature as he perceived it. What he perceived about human nature, at least in his economic essays, was that people act rationally in response to economic incentives.

Even more interesting than Locke's assumption that individuals act in response to their own economic self-interest is his apparent attitude that such behavior is not necessarily reprehensible, even when economic self-interest may involve breaking (or avoiding) civil laws governing economic behavior.[19] Rather, at least in the specific case of price-fixing by the civil authorities, Locke criticizes the state for passing bad laws in the first place, laws which force basically honest men to become criminals in order to conduct their business.[20] The implication is that since prices are determined by natural laws, price regulation is bad legislation and individuals are not to be blamed for avoiding it where they can: natural economic laws take precedence over civil economic laws just as natural law takes precedence over all civil law. Thus the government is limited in its ability to control economic phenomena both practically and morally: practically in that any attempt to legislate contrary to economic laws is doomed to the failure of unexpected, adverse consequences, and morally in that governments should not pass laws which contradict natural laws.

Locke makes another argument against price-fixing, however, one which puts a further limitation on the government's ability (and right) to control the economy and one which incidentally supports his theory of property in the *Second Treatise*. Locke argues that if the interest rate is lowered, it will "transfer a third part of the monied man's estate, who has nothing else to live on into the merchant's pocket; and that without any merit in the one, or transgression in the other." He continues, "Private men's interests ought not thus to be neglected, nor sacrificed to any thing but the manifest advantage of the public."[21] Locke makes this same argument in several places, that price controls result in a redistribution of wealth which penalizes some and rewards others with no real benefit accruing to the kindgom. Since the purpose of government is to protect legitimate property, Locke's position that government has no right to pass legislation which will arbitrarily confiscate some people's property and transfer it to others is understandable. If he believes that the prices determined in the marketplace are the result of natural laws, then the income earned in market transactions is legitimate property which the government is charged with protecting. In the state of nature property was earned by the application of labor to unowned natural resources, but in the advanced economy characteristic of civil

118

society property is earned through commercial activity which takes place in organized markets. These commercial activities are based on contractual arrangements among individuals to exchange goods (or lend money) and an attempt to change these contracts would "void bargains lawfully made, and give to Richard what is Peter's due."[22] Clearly such arbitrary action is not within the legitimate confines of government activity, since it is exactly counter to the purpose for which government is formed. Price regulation is therefore unacceptable except in cases where there is a clear advantage to the public.

While Locke never explains what might constitute an advantage to the public clear enough to justify price-fixing, perhaps we may infer from his arguments on the subject that if it would improve trade rather than disrupt it, he might find price-fixing acceptable. Consider, for example, the following passage concerning the potential effect on land values of the change in the rate of interest. Here he again mentions the redistribution of income, but changes his emphasis:

> This indeed a little alters the distribution of the money we have amongst us Englishmen here at home, but neither helps to continue what we have, nor brings in more from abroad: Which being the only concernment of the Kingdom, in reference to its wealth, is apt to be supposed by us without doors to be the only care of a Parliament. For it matters not, so it be here amongst us, whether the money be in Thomas or Richard's hands, provided it be so ordered that, whoever has it, may be encouraged to let it go into the current of trade, for the improvement of the general stock, and wealth of the nation.[23]

This attitude can be found throughout *Some Considerations*, where time and time again policies are evaluated with respect to whether or not they help or hinder trade.[24] Here, then, it seems Locke is describing a positive role for the government in the economy, to encourage trade. But when one searches Locke's writings for proposals on how the government might actually do this, one finds very little. Locke's major contribution to economic policy-making seems to be in *Some Considerations,* where he advised the government not to do something, in particular, not to lower the legal rate of interest. Furthermore, Locke's interest policy is indicative of his whole attitude toward the government's ability to control or regulate the economy as revealed in both *Some Considerations* and *Further Considerations.* Aside from several suggestions about specific kinds of taxes that can be levied, Locke makes few positive recommendations for laws to control economic variables. An obvious exception would seem to be interest rate regulation, which he believes is necessary to counteract the city bankers' monopoly, but even here the monopoly was made possible in the first place by bad government policy.[25] His attitude is generally that a low rate of interest, gold inflows, and abundant supplies of skilled labor are all beneficial to the economy, but that they can be achieved only through economic action and not through political action. Any attempt to bring them about through legislation will only compound the problems the government wants to solve. The key to his reasoning is revealed when he says, "I grant low interest, where all men consent to it, is an advantage to trade."[26] Prices are arrived at ultimately by the voluntary consent of the participants in the marketplace. It is a form of consent which takes precedence over the government's right to make laws, not only in a legal sense but, more importantly, in a functional sense. That is, people usually act in such a way as to make the civil laws concerning the economy inoperative, and hence they are not giving their consent to the legislation. The government can make laws concerning property only with the consent of the governed because it can rule only with the consent of the governed.

In Locke's social thought, it appears that the government is relegated to playing a passive role in the domestic economy.

Government can provide a system of civil laws to regulate property disputes,[27] maintain a stable money supply,[28] and tax its citizens with their consent to finance its activities,[29] but otherwise it cannot confiscate property without some overriding urgency justified by the public good (unfortunately, Locke does not define "public good"). The government is established in large part to make economic activity possible and to make the enjoyment of the fruits of economic activity more secure. It is the servant of the economy, which is nothing more than the property-generating activities of the individuals in a society.

We have painted a picture so far of Locke the classical economic liberal. While his political liberalism is well known, his economic liberalism has often been overlooked. Now this analysis must be qualified somewhat. Although it has been shown that Locke describes surprisingly little for the government to do to control or direct the economy, it would be an exaggeration to claim that Locke was therefore an advocate of a policy of laissez-faire. While there is nothing in Locke's main economic or political writings which would be inconsistent with a policy of laissez-faire, he was responsible for writing some shorter political position papers which tell quite a different story. For instance, one has only to read his version of a reform of the poor laws to see a side of him that is not evident in his more scholarly works, for he argues for restrictions on labor mobility, involuntary conscription of the poor, and compulsory child labor in government workhouses.[30] Even the argument that his reforms were aimed at making the poor self-sufficient does not justify from the classical liberal perspective such direct government control of individual behavior. In addition, in his recommendations concerning the Irish linen trade, he advocates forcibly supplanting the Irish woolen industry which was competing with England with a linen industry which would not.[31] Clearly, here Locke displays no penchant for letting the laws of economics regulate trade. While it is possible that Locke had one set of policies for the domestic economy and one for a subordinate colony, still it is evident that Locke did not subscribe to a policy of laissez-faire when he wrote these proposals. Perhaps we can attribute the difference in attitude to the difference between Locke the politician and Locke the social scientist. The position papers were not serious attempts at social theory and perhaps we should therefore discount their importance in his thought.

Letwin has argued more definitely that Locke was not an advocate of a policy of laissez-faire, that in fact "he was very much an advocate of government intervention in economic affairs"; this argument is based not only on the evidence of Locke's poor law reform and the Irish linen trade recommendation but on Locke's "repeated insistence in the *Considerations* that the government must regulate trade in order to assure a proper balance of trade."[32] While we have not found examples of this "repeated insistence" on government intervention to assure a proper balance of trade,[33] the question is still open as to how far Locke approached a philosophy of laissez-faire. Letwin claims that a belief that the economy functioned according to natural laws does not necessarily imply a philosophy of laissez-faire unless one believes that nature left to itself produces an ideal state, or at least a state which is preferable to that created by "special interests and the bungling of men who set about to improve on nature's work."[34] Such a belief, however, if it is not to rest solely on "inane optimism," requires a notion of a natural tendency toward equilibrium and an explanation of how equilibrium comes about, notions he claims Locke did not have.

We have shown in the foregoing analysis that Locke did explain equilibrium market prices and at least alluded to the process by which these prices are reached. It was precisely his belief in the importance of allowing prices to adjust to equilibrium levels which led to his criticism of government attempts at price-fixing. Insofar as a policy of laissez-faire requires an economic theory of general equilibrium, Letwin is clearly correct. There is no evidence that Locke ever thought of anything remotely resembling a general equilibrium for an economy as a whole in his economic essays. Yet it is too damning to conclude that Locke's antagonism toward government interference in markets was based on inane optimism. (It is doubtful that Locke could ever have been called an optimist.) He did not, for example, believe in a harmony of interests: in fact, he describes several instances where, in the face of economic distress, various segments of society will be at each other's throats. It was the duty of the government to order the economy so that such economic distress never occurs. He did believe, however, that in the specific instances with which he was familiar, direct government interference in markets would "prejudice and inconvenience trade, and put ...affairs out of order."[35] Clearly Locke believed that the market was superior to the "bungling of men" that Letwin refers to. The reasons for his belief were based partly on empirical observation and, interestingly, partly on a notion of justice that gives indirect support to his understanding of the benefits of permitting the "natural course of things" in the economy to find their way.

## THE JUST PRICE

Locke's ideas on justice in the marketplace can be found in an entry in his commonplace book dated 1695, entitled *Venditio*. It is especially interesting here not only because it explicitly deals with the problem of justice in exchange, but also because it supports Schumpeter's view of Locke as a Protestant Scholastic. *Venditio* is not well known in the Locke literature. We have found no references to it in any of the treatments of Locke's economics and only one reference to it in the literature on Locke's political theory. That reference was in an article published in 1968 by John Dunn, "Justice and Locke's Political Theory," in which Dunn also published for the first time the text of *Venditio*.[36] It is unfortunate that this short piece has been overlooked for so long, since it is the only place we know of in which Locke directly examines the moral aspects of economic behavior. It is especially interesting to historians of economic thought because the attitudes displayed in the note are very much those of the century to follow, while the style of the piece illustrates clearly Locke's links to the Scholastic world.

Locke's attitude toward the marketplace is made evident from the opening lines of the note:

> Upon demand what is the measure that ought to regulate the price for which anyone sells so as to keep it within the bounds of equity and justice. I suppose it in short to be this, the market price at the place where he sells. Whosoever keeps to that in whatever he sells I think is free from cheat, extortion or oppression or any guilt in whatever he sells supposing no fallacy in his wares.[37]

He then goes on for two pages to clarify his meaning by examining the ethics of pricing under a variety of circumstances.

Locke's reasons for suggesting that the market price is the just price take two forms. The first is the familiar argument of *Some Considerations* that if one attempted to sell at a price other then the market price, human behavior is such that one's ends in so doing would be thwarted. The second argument is the new one that the market price fulfills the requirements for justice, and therefore it is immoral to sell at another price. We see both arguments in the cases he discusses to illustrate his view of the just price.

The first problem Locke chooses to discuss is the following: suppose the price of wheat increases from five shillings per bushel last year to ten shillings per bushel this year. Is it just for a wheat merchant to sell what amounts to identical wheat at a higher price this year then he would have sold it at last year? The answer, of course, is that it is perfectly just to sell at the higher price this year,[38] for the following reasons:

1. If a wheat merchant attempted to sell his wheat this year at last year's prices, another would "buy up his corn at this low rate and sell it again to others at the market rate and so they make a profit of his weakness and share a part of his money."[39] Obviously, the opportunity for economic gain provides an incentive for individuals to engage in arbitrage, with the only result being that the arbitragers get some of the income which otherwise would have gone to the wheat seller. The implication is that the arbitragers have no more, and probably less, right to the income from the sale of the wheat than the wheat merchant does.

2. But what if the same merchant decides, out of a sense of charity, to sell only to the poor at a lower price than the market price? Locke answers that "this indeed is charity, but not what strict justice requires," because if it is unjust to sell to a poor man at ten shillings per bushel, it is equally unjust to sell to a rich man at the same price, "for justice has but one measure for all men." (This, by the way, is Locke's only attempt to define justice. Obviously his concern here is with commutative rather than distributive justice.)

3. If the merchant still wishes to sell below the market price, and to avoid resale decides to sell only to consumers and not to "jobbers and ingrossers" (arbitragers), he still would be doomed to failure because, given the limits of human knowledge, he has no way of distinguishing those who would resell the wheat from those who would not.

4. And finally, to the argument that it is immoral to sell wheat at a higher price one year than another because the physical commodity has not changed in the two years and hence is worth the same (the argument that the wheat's intrinsic value does not change), Locke answers: "it is worth no more tis true in its natural value because it will not feed more men nor better feed them than it did last year, but yet it is worth more in its political and merchant value as I may so call it, which lies in the proportion of the quantity of wheat to the proportion of money in that place and the need of one

and the other.''[40] Notice that Locke is making the same argument about value that he made in *Some Considerations.* Things may have an ''intrinsic value'' because of their ability to aid human life, but their economic value depends only partly on the intrinsic value and is also a result of the quantity for sale; it is the economic value which is important to the determination of price.[41]

The moral principle established by Locke so far is that justice requires that everyone be treated alike and therefore the market price is the just price because it applies equally to all men.[42] Anyone who violates this principle by selling at one price to one person and at another price to someone else violates the principle of justice: ''He that makes use of another's fancy or necessity to sell ribbon or cloth etc. dearer to him to another man at the same time, cheats him.''[43] All forms of price discrimination, then, are unjust because price discrimination is a means of profiting from differences in the demand for a product between different people.[44]

But what of those situations where a market price is not established for a particular article? What is the just price then? Or even more difficult, what is the just price when one person wants to buy something from another who has not intended to sell the article in the first place? One cannot refer to the market price because the seller has not put his commodity on the market. Locke uses several cases of this nature to emphasize the criterion he has established for justice in exchange, and in each case a just price is established when the seller determines what the article is worth to him, regardless of what the market value of the good in question might otherwise be.[45] The buyer then has the choice of either paying what the seller asks or not buying the good at all. The only limitation on the price the seller may ask is that he must not take advantage of any special need or desire on the part of the buyer in order to ask more than the thing is worth to himself. He must set a price that he would be willing to sell at to anyone, not just the person who actually wants the item.

What is interesting to an economist in this discussion is that Locke allows no room for a bargaining process in these cases of isolated exchange. While it is apparent that in his criterion for a just exchange in such cases, Locke is trying to duplicate the just features of the marketplace, in fact what he accomplishes is to make the subjective evaluation of the seller determine the selling price, while the subjective evaluation of the buyer must be conscientiously ignored by the seller if he is to be just. One wonders why Locke did not consider it to be an equally just arrangement for the buyer to decide what the article was worth to him and then offer the seller that price. Why is the seller's subjective evaluation more of a guide to value and hence to the just price than the buyer's?

The answer is that if each buyer were to offer a price to the seller, there would be many different prices for the same good, implying that it had more than one value, whereas to Locke the most attractive feature of the marketplace was that only one price prevailed in any one place at any one time and hence all people were treated equally. If the seller decides on the price he is willing to sell at (Locke calls this his "own market rate"), then all potential buyers face the same price and the market is more closely duplicated: "what anyone has he may value at what rate he will and transgresses not against justice if he sells it at any price provided he makes no distinction of buyers but parts with it as cheap to this as he would to any other buyer."[46] Obviously, Locke does not understand the more modern idea that if both parties to a transaction freely agree to a price, both gain from the exchange. Recognition of the gains from trade was still a century off.

While justice is the primary concern in regulating the exchange between individuals, Locke also makes it clear that charity may also be involved from time to time. It is perfectly just to sell one's wares at whatever price the market determines, yet there may be circumstances where charity may require action that goes beyond the requirements of strict justice. Locke illustrates this proposition by comparing two towns, one where there is no famine and wheat sells at five shillings per bushel, and another where famine reigns and wheat sells at twenty shillings per bushel. Locke sees no injustice in a merchant's selling his wheat in the famine-ridden land at a price four times that in the other land, "because he sells at the market rate at the place where he is, but sells no dearer to Thomas then he would to Richard." But the seller's profit-maximizing behavior must not go so far as to permit the inhabitants of the famine-stricken land to starve to death. It is acceptable to sell the wheat at the highest price possible

> yet if he carry it away unless they will give him more than they are able, or extorts so much from their present necessity as not to leave them the means of subsistence afterwards he offends against the common rule of charity as a man and if they perish any of them by reason of extortion is no doubt guilty of murder. For though all selling merchants' gain arises only from the advantage he makes of the buyer's want whether it be a want of necessity or fancy 'tis all one yet he must not make use of his necessity to his destruction, and enrich himself so as to make another perish. . . . he is bound to be at some loss and impart of his own to save another from perishing.[47]

While justice requires that all men be treated equally, charity goes beyond justice when a life is at stake and requires a positive act to save that life.[48] In this extreme case Locke obviously does not consider the market-clearing function of price to be important. He is concerned more with the manner in which the seller gains from selling his wheat.

The last point for discussion found in *Venditio* is for our purposes also the most important, and that is Locke's too brief treatment of the just profit. Here too we find evidence that Locke believed that the market treats all people equally and therefore justly, but in addition we find that he believed that the market eventually leads to equal benefits for all participants, an entirely different proposition, and one that presages a concept of general equilibrium. Locke's main point is that if the market price at the place of sale is the just price, then there can be no way of determining a just profit. The implication is that profits depend upon both the price received and the cost of bringing the good to sale. If the just profit were limited to, say, five or ten per cent, the buyer would have to know the cost of the commodity to the seller before a just price could be settled upon. This is clearly impossible for two reasons: costs differ from seller to seller for the same good and the buyer has no way of knowing what costs his particular seller has incurred; even if it were possible to know these costs, setting a fixed percentage profit for the seller would result in many different prices for the same good.[49] In the face of varying costs, there are not enough degrees of freedom to set both a just price and a just profit.

Locke further argues that there is another reason why it is unreasonable to set a limit to the just profit: sellers must take their chances with both gains and losses, and if their gains are limited to some fixed percentage but their losses are not, they will eventually go out of business. ''This obligation to certain loss often, without certainty of reparation will quickly put an end to merchandising.''[50] While Locke's prediction of the consequence of limiting the profit rate was certainly too extreme, he was basically correct that a reduction in the return to mercantile activities would at least reduce the number of merchants.

Finally, and most importantly for our purposes, Locke implies that in the long run the question of a just profit is irrelevant; that if the market is allowed to function, the result will be that everyone is treated fairly, because the gains and losses will eventually cancel each other out:

> The measure that is common to buyer and seller is just that if one should buy as cheap as he could in the

market the other should sell as dear as he could there, everyone running his venture and taking his chances which by *the mutual and perpetually changing wants of money and commodities in buyer and seller comes to a pretty equal and fair account.*[51] [Italics mine]

In this important passage, Locke seems to be saying that prices are subject to frequent change as they respond to changes in the tastes and desires of economic actors.[52] These price changes affect the fortunes of sellers such that a profit one day may easily and unpredictably turn into a loss the next. There is no need to be concerned about the seller's receiving a just profit, however, because in the long run all sellers will earn approximately equal returns. Once again, the market is just, this time because sellers as well as buyers are treated equally. While this is not exactly the harmony-of-interest doctrine—that is, Locke does not claim that each man pursuing his own self-interest will, as if by an invisible hand, be drawn to serve the best interests of society[53]—he does say that each man pursuing his own self-interest is acting justly and in turn receives just treatment in the marketplace. Furthermore, that justice, coupled with the responsiveness of the market to change, assures that in the long run no one will be harmed by other people's pursuing their own self-interest.

This is admittedly scanty evidence for attributing some early notion of general equilibrium to Locke, since all he really says is that in the long run no one enterprise will be any more profitable than any other, without explaining why this should be so. But his discussion of the just profit does lend added support to his skepticism toward the government's ability to control economic phenomena. In addition to his argument that people will not tolerate legislation which operates against their economic self-interest (the argument of *Some Considerations*), in *Venditio* he emphasizes the limitations of all human foresight in a changing market, limitations which would make it difficult for a government to respond to changing economic parameters. Hence the consequences of government regulation of the market are less desirable than the results obtained by the unregulated market (this is the sophisticated argument in favor of laissez-faire that Letwin claims Locke was not equipped to make). Furthermore, in *Venditio* he also makes the moral argument in the Scholastic spirit that market prices are just prices, and the more sweeping claim that market activities lead to just results. Apparently, Locke is suggesting that the market guarantees both commutative and distributive justice.

While Locke used both scientific and moral arguments to support his view of the limitations of government in both the political and economic realms, it was the scientific arguments which he emphasized. Government power, both political and economic, is limited by the tolerance of the citizens it governs. It is of great significance to the development of social science that the limitations which Locke recognized were imposed by a natural order which, although ultimately dictated by God, was immediately determined by human nature and its subset, human rationality. If social science is characterized by an attempt to explain human social interaction in a systematic way based on assumptions about the characteristics of individual human beings, we can conclude that Locke was a social scientist who in his economic and political writings was presenting a consistent, integrated view of society.

# SIX

# CONCLUSION

JOHN LOCKE WAS an important contributor to the development of economic analysis. Although he has from time to time been classified as a mercantilist because of his concern with national wealth and specie inflows, this represents but one aspect of his work, and he was by no means one of these partisan pamphleteers. As William Letwin has argued, Locke can be more properly categorized as one of the originators of scientific economics.[1]

The basis of Locke's description of the economic system was a theory of price determination which relied heavily on both Aristotelian doctrine and current scientific language for its formation. He defined prices as barter prices determined by comparing the proportions between the quantities and the vents of the goods bartered, and money as a special case of commodities in general which served as the numeraire for all the others. The value of money, too, was determined by the proportion of its quantity to its vent, but, because of its special position, its vent was constant and its value depended on its quantity alone—this was the basis for his quantity theory of money. An integral part of this quantity theory was the concept of the velocity of money, a concept which Locke

132

used to explain the determination of the price level and the level of trade. He understood how money was part of a circular flow of goods and money throughout the economy. Although Locke probably had no idea that this system of price determination based upon a series of proportions would under certain conditions tend toward an efficient allocation of resources, he did believe that market prices were equilibrium prices which enabled trade to take place in the least costly way.

Locke's strength as an economist came from his ability to use his set of economic principles to identify certain important prices and explain how they functioned in a macro- as well as a microeconomic framework. Specifically, he showed how interest rates, rents, and foreign exchange rates were all in themselves prices subject to the laws of quantity and vent, and therefore could not be arbitrarily dictated by governmental fiat. Within this framework, he gave consistent evaluations of the determinants of the quantity and vent of each of these prices and tried to show how a law to lower the rate of interest would have adverse effects on either the quantity or vent of each one. A picture emerges of an economic scientist devising his theories from his personal observations and then applying his principles to specific situations.

Locke was not only a scientist, however; he was also a philosopher. In addition to establishing a set of scientific laws according to which the operation of the economy could be predicted, Locke also tried to establish the philosophical foundation for these laws. Moreover, in the course of attempting to establish the morality of individualistic political behavior, he also attempted to establish the morality of economic behavior. Political society he conceived of as a means to protect economic achievement and hence as subordinate to it. He began by defining natural law and natural rights, showing in the *Second Treatise* how natural rights implied a natural right to private property, and finally describing in detail why the right to own private property is necessary for the economic well-being of mankind. In the course of these arguments, he identified labor as the source of value and illustrated the productivity of roundabout means of production. He gave an account of the origin of money based on natural, voluntary behavior and showed that a consequence of its use was an unequal distribution of wealth, ultimately leading to the necessity of forming civil society. Thus the economy was described as a prepolitical institution that arose out of the natural actions of moral men, while political society was necessitated both by the immoral behavior of covetous men who made the enjoyment of property insecure and by the problems encountered in defining property rights under conditions of land scarcity. Economic society provides not only the source of political society, but also its major aim and sustenance. It is the means of maintaining continuity in social relations during times of political stress.

Whether or not Locke can be considered to have been an early social scientist, where social science implies explaining the consequences of human action on the basis of assumptions about the unique characteristics of human beings, is a difficult problem. In both Locke's economic and his political writings, he assumed that individuals behaved rationally in response to economic incentives so as to further their own economic self-interest, and further, he did not identify this as reprehensible behavior. This pursuit of economic gain is the basis for Locke's emphasis on the limitations of government in both the political and the economic spheres. Specifically, he argued that government could not arbitrarily confiscate the property of its citizens since it was originally formed by them to protect their property, and since they would not tolerate government action contrary to that purpose. Furthermore, government was limited in its ability to control economic variables for two reasons: it was powerless to do so, because economic laws were equivalent in their significance to laws of the physical universe; and it was morally restrained from doing so, because its interference would reduce or arbitrarily transfer property from one citizen to another. But it is also true that Locke's view of the ultimate morality of the marketplace, where competitive market prices were just prices and the interaction of buyers and sellers guaranteed that all participants in the market would be treated justly, indicated that although he may have been a social scientist in his view of how the economy and the polity functioned, he also retained the medieval concern with the justice of the social system.

The modern reader might find the different roles which Locke played in his writings on the economy somewhat difficult to reconcile: British patriot attempting to discover wherein lie the best interests of the kingdom in terms of wealth, power, and sustained economic growth; value-free scientist searching for the basic principles of one form of social action; philosopher attempting to lay the moral foundations of economic society. All three, however, are completely reconcilable given Locke's idea of society based on natural law. As William Letwin points out, "by the seventeenth century, 'law of nature' had come to include two disparate notions, moral laws and scientific laws."[2] Both of these concepts were united by the single common thread: the belief that a Christian God guaranteed the content of both. God gave men a benevolent universe wherein physical things were required to obey scientific laws of nature, and at the same time men were required to obey the dictates of a natural moral law. Both kinds of natural law were known to men through their reason, and they had only to discover and live according to both in order to live a godly life. It was not at all unlikely, then, that a man of science should be concerned with improving the wealth of the nation and determining the morality of human behavior in addition to searching for regularities in nature, since all would require the same kind of mental activity and all would be aimed at the same end: discovering the inherent order and benevolence in God's world. One has only to look at the careers of men like Robert Boyle and Isaac Newton to realize that Locke was not alone in this triple concern, although Locke was far more involved in the practical and moral realm than they.

Since Locke was more a social scientist than a physical scientist, his range of inquiry was somewhat more circumscribed than that of the physical scientist. He endeavored to lay bare the laws of economic and political behavior in order to show men how best to achieve their justifiable aim of economic well-being. If at times he seemed to be operating from the mercantilist premise of wealth for England above all, it was only because this, too, was in accordance with his idea of natural law. Each country existed in a state of nature with every other, but although there was no common civil law to control their actions, it was in the best interests of each country to uphold the economic contracts permitting trade and commerce to take place, just as it had been to the advantage of the individual in the state of nature to form economic contracts before there were common civil laws to uphold them. And just as in the state of nature the most industrious individual was able to amass the greatest fortune, so in the international state of nature, the most industrious and wisely administered country would become the wealthiest and most powerful. Locke saw it as his duty to show England how she could be this most industrious and powerful country.

Thus it was that Locke, who seemed to write from an essentially mercantilist point of view, was able to accomplish much more than any mercantilist writer had done. He was able, by adopting a disinterested, scientific approach to his subject, to arrive at a set of principles describing the behavior of essential economic variables and thereby to provide men with more reliable knowledge of how to increase their national wealth. Although the theories he formulated were eventually replaced with even more powerful theories, he left us something much more important than any one particular theory: he bequeathed to economics an attitude and a method of approach which did much to make our discipline into a science.

# NOTES

CHAPTER 1

1. The major sources for the following biographical sketch are Maurice Cranston, *John Locke: A Biography;* H. R. Fox-Bourne, *The Life of John Locke,* 2 vols.; Kenneth Dewhurst, *John Locke: Physician and Philosopher;* William Letwin, *The Origins of Scientific Economics,* pp. 158–84; and Patrick H. Kelly, *Locke on Money* (manuscript).

2. Fox-Bourne, 1:40.

3. Quoted in Fox-Bourne, 1:61.

4. Fox-Bourne, 1:49.

5. John Locke, *Essays on the Law of Nature,* ed. W. Von Leyden, p. 35.

6. J. W. Gough, *John Locke's Political Philosophy,* 2d ed., p. 1.

7. Among them are Joseph A. Schumpeter, *History of Economic Analysis,* p. 117; and James Bonar, *Philosophy and Political Economy,* p. 98. The influence of Aristotle on Locke's economic theories will be explored in greater detail here in subsequent chapters.

8. Von Leyden, ed., *Essays,* p. 82.

9. On the origins of the Royal Society, see Margery Purver, *The Royal Society: Concept and Creation.*

10. Cranston, *John Locke,* p. 197.

11. Quoted in Dewhurst, p. 38.

12. A version of this early paper has been published in Letwin, *Origins*, pp. 295–323.

13. Letwin, *Origins*, p. 168.

14. Ibid., p. 171.

15. It is also possible that he left England in order to disassociate himself from Shaftesbury and any political maneuvering during this dangerous time.

16. This hypothesis is presented by Peter Laslett in the introduction to his excellent edition of Locke's *Two Treatises of Government*, 2d ed. chap. 3, pp. 45–66; and by Cranston, *John Locke*, pp. 207–8.

17. Letwin, *Origins*, p. 178.

18. Reprinted in *Several Papers Relating to Money, Interest and Trade, Etc.* Hereafter cited as *Some Considerations*. This account of the publication of *Some Considerations* is taken from Kelly, pp. 30–31.

19. Quoted in Letwin, *Origins*, p. 179.

20. Reprinted in *Several Papers*. Hereafter cited as *Further Considerations*.

21. Locke's role in influencing recoinage of silver at full value is explored by Laslett in "John Locke, the Great Recoinage, and the Origins of the Board of Trade," pp. 370–92; and more recently by Kelly, pp. 37–51.

22. The "scattered papers" all remained unpublished during Locke's lifetime. They include: *Notes on Trade*, 1674; *For a General Naturalization*, 1693; *Labor*, 1693; and *Venditio*, 1695. On these papers, see Kelly.

CHAPTER 2

1. This is not meant to suggest that Locke actually formulated a theory of value first and then consciously set out to apply it to current economic problems. Kelly (p. 86) has shown that in the actual preparation of the manuscript, the sections on value were added on almost as an afterthought. Rather, I believe that Locke was led to enunciate a theory of value to explain the underlying premise of his theories of money, interest, and trade. He seems to have reasoned backward from particular applications toward a general principle rather than forward from a general principle to particular applications.

2. This is true not only of Locke, but of most seventeenth-century writers. Footnoting is a mania of our age of widespread literacy. In earlier times, it was taken for granted that the reading public, which was small, was well enough educated to be able to supply the source of nonoriginal ideas. Only the really obscure writers tended to be credited for their ideas. (From Josef Soudek in personal correspondence.)

3. Although Locke's collection of economic tracts was "magnificent by contemporary standards," according to Kelly, referring to Richard Ashcraft's work on Locke's library ("John Locke's Library: Portrait of an Intellectual," *Transactions of the Cambridge Bibliographical Society* 5 (1969): 47–60), most of these were acquired only after the publication of *Some Considerations* and long after the bulk of the essay was actually written. See John Harrison and Peter Laslett, *The Library of John Locke,* p. 25; and Letwin, *Origins,* p. 168.

4. See *Politics* 1. 9. I have used the Penguin Classics edition, translated by J. A. Sinclair.

5. For a detailed discussion of the value theory of the Scholastics, see Bernard W. Dempsey, "Just Price in a Functional Economy," reprinted in *Essays in Economic Thought: Aristotle to Marshall,* ed. Joseph J. Spengler and William R. Allen, pp. 45–60; Raymond De Roover, "The Concept of the Just Price: Theory and Economic Policy," reprinted in *Readings in the History of Economic Theory,* ed. Ingrid H. Rima, pp. 9–21; and Schumpeter, pp. 82–107. On value theory in seventeenth-century mercantilist writing, see Marian Bowley, "Some Seventeenth Century Contributions to the Theory of Value," pp. 125–26. Letwin (*Origins,* p. 224) suggests that the paradox of value, although known "since time immemorial, probably entered the stream of economic theory through Locke's *Considerations.*"

6. *Some Considerations,* p. 66.

7. *Second Treatise,* in *Two Treatises,* ed. Laslett, p. 312.

8. *Some Considerations,* p. 67.

9. This is the common textbook description found among others in Eric Roll, *A History of Economic Thought,* 3d ed. p. 115; and Henry W. Spiegel, *The Growth of Economic Thought,* p. 162. This is also the description of Locke's value theory offered by Letwin (*Origins,* p. 190).

141

10. Bowley, "Some Seventeenth Century Contributions," p. 124. Marjorie Grice-Hutchinson (*The School of Salamanca*, p. 27) claims that the role of scarcity in determining price was described by Saint Thomas in the thirteenth century and known to all subsequent Schoolmen; and Dempsey ("Just Price," p. 57) attributes an understanding of scarcity to Duns Scotus (1265–1308).

11. Nicholas Barbon, *A Discourse of Trade,* cited in Letwin, *Origins,* p. 60.

12. Dudley North, *Discourses upon Trade* (1690).

13. Bowley, "Some Seventeenth Century Contributions," p. 130. This implies that vent would correspond only to quantity demanded at equilibrium prices, which would make Locke's analysis useless to explain price changes.

14. "All things that are bought and solde, raise and fall their price in proportion, as there are more buyers or sellers. Where there are a great many sellers to a few buyers . . . the things to be sold will be cheap. On the other side, turn the tables and raise up a great many buyers for a few sellers, and the same thing will immediately grow dear" (*Some Considerations,* pp. 59–60).

15. Ibid., p. 14.

16. Ibid., p. 45.

17. Ibid., p. 46.

18. Ibid.

19. While it may appear that Locke overstates the lack of influence of intrinsic value on price, in fact his purpose is to emphasize that the only way that changes in economic parameters will affect price is by operating on either the quantity or the vent of a commodity.

20. *Some Considerations,* p. 46.

21: If Locke meant that *demand* in the neoclassical sense for necessities was totally inelastic, then in order for a market price to be determinate, the supply schedule would have to be upward sloping, and "scarcity" here would mean a supply schedule rather than a given quantity. It is highly unlikely that this was the way Locke understood price determination, however. As we shall see below, Locke described price determination as a proportion between quantity and vent. In the case of necessities, then, he probably reasoned as follows: the vent of necessities is constant at some level, so price is determined by the quantity alone. This is much the same way as he explained why the value of money was determined by quantity alone.

22. *Some Considerations*, p. 47.

23. Ibid., p. 48. This description illustrates the principle that the demand for a general category of goods (food in this case) is always less elastic than the demand for any particular good within the category (wheat and oats here).

24. Ibid., p. 94.

25. Ibid., p. 95. Cf. Pufendorf, *De Jure Naturae et Gentium*, 2:681–81. It is interesting that the idea that there is a set of luxury (or prestige) goods that allegedly refute the law of demand persists even today in some quarters.

26. Locke was not the first to note the role of substitutes in determining the price elasticity of demand. Sir William Petty states: "But forasmuch as almost all Commodities have their substitutes or Succedanea, and that almost all uses may be answered several ways; and for that novelty, surprize, example of Superiors, and opinion of unexaminable effects do adde or take away from the price of things, we must adde these contingent Causes to the permanent Causes above mentioned, in the judicious foresight and computation whereof lies the excellency of a Merchant" (*Economic Writings of Sir William Petty,* ed. C. H. Hull, 1:90). The permanent causes involve the amount of labor necessary to produce the product and the number of "Supernumerary Interlopers into any trade over and above all that are necessary." Petty did not describe the various kinds of goods or how the number of substitutes affect the price of the product in the degree of detail which Locke supplied.

27. *Some Considerations*, p. 96.

28. Ibid., p. 67.

29. Ibid., p. 68.

30. Ibid., p. 70.

31. Ibid., pp. 61, 67.

32. Ibid., p. 72.

33. Josef Soudek, "Aristotle's Theory of Exchange," pp. 45–75. Soudek, in his original and far-reaching study, has shown that Aristotle's theory of exchange was a sophisticated attempt to use mathematical reasoning to explain how essentially unlike things can be made equivalent to one another in an act of exchange. Aristotle

explained an exchange of equivalent values in terms of a theory of proportionate reciprocity which he represented by a complex geometric proportion composed of four ratios. The component parts of the ratios were the skills of the parties to the trade and their respective wants for both the goods they have initially and those they are trying to acquire. Proportionate reciprocity was achieved when the satisfaction of both parties before and after the exchange is in proportion to the goods exchanged. Soudek has also convincingly argued that Aristotle's theory of exchange was badly misunderstood during the Middle Ages and into the present, so if Locke was at all inspired by Aristotle's formulation, the inspiration must have been limited to the form of the analysis rather than the substance.

34. See Soudek, pp. 64–68, and S. Todd Lowry, "Aristotle's Mathematical Analysis of Exchange," pp. 44–66.

35. For a good description of the achievements of seventeenth-century science, see A. C. Crombie, *Medieval and Early Modern Science*, vol. 2; and Herbert Butterfield, *The Origins of Modern Science 1300–1800*.

36. William Letwin would disagree with this. He states, in his *Origins of Scientific Economics*, "His interest in science left no discernible trace in Locke's economic writings" (p. 167). It is our contention that Letwin has overlooked an important factor in Locke's thought.

37. *Some Considerations*, pp. 63–64.

38. Ibid., p. 63.

39. Ibid., p. 66.

40. Ibid., p. 52. See also pp. 61–62: "The value of anything, compared with itself or with a standing measure is greater, as its quantity is less in proportion to its vent: But in comparing it or exchanging it with any other thing, the quantity and vent of that thing too must be allowed for, in the computation of their value.

41. Ibid., p. 45.

42. *Second Treatise*, pp. 311–12.

43. Ibid., p. 308.

44. Here is an apparent similarity between Locke and Aristotle. In book 1, chapter 9 of the *Politics*, Aristotle describes money as arising out of an agreement among men to use some convenient material such as iron or silver as a medium of exchange. For Locke,

however, the "agreement" is not explicit but evolves through time as men adapt their institutions to the constraints they face. See below, chapter 5.

45. *Politics* 1. 9 (p. 42).

46. *Some Considerations,* p. 31.

47. Ibid.

48. *Further Considerations,* pp. 4, 9.

49. *Some Considerations,* p. 29. It is not clear how Locke would have responded to the argument, made by several of his contemporaries, that men do in fact accept paper (or token coins) as money. He simply denied the empirical validity of such a contention.

50. Most of *Further Considerations* is devoted to this idea.

51. *Further Considerations,* p. 4.

52. *Some Considerations,* p. 31.

53. *Further Considerations,* p. 11.

54. Arthur E. Monroe (*Monetary Theory before Adam Smith,* p. 113) points out that in spite of the superiority of Locke's quantity theory, it was the metallist aspects of it that most impressed his contemporaries, and the importance of the theory itself was overlooked for more than thirty years.

55. "Money therefore in buying and selling being perfectly in the same condition with other commodities, and subject to the same Laws of Value" (*Some Considerations,* p. 55).

56. Ibid., p. 71. See also p. 62: "The desire for money is constantly almost everywhere the same, its vent varies very little"; and p. 75: "its [money's] vent is the same."

57. Excellent sources on the origins of the quantity theory are Hugo Hegeland, *The Quantity Theory of Money,* pp. 15–31; A. W. Marget, *The Theory of Price,* vol. 1; Monroe, *Monetary Theory,* pp. 108–14 and pp. 53–60; and Schumpeter, pp. 311–17.

58. Grice-Hutchinson, p. 52.

59. Schumpeter (p. 314) calls this "simple metallism."

60. Monroe, *Monetary Theory,* pp. 100–106; Schumpeter, p. 314.

61. *Some Considerations,* pp. 78–79 and p. 114.

62. Ibid., p. 73. The fact that money could alter in value at all was a source of displeasure to Locke. He would have preferred that the standard of value be unchanging rather than subject to the

accidents of mining discoveries, to which end he considered several alternatives. Specifically, he suggested wheat as a more reliable measure of value for a long period of time, since "it keeps the nearest proportion to its consumption (which is more studied and designed in this than other commodities) of anything, if you take it for seven or twenty years together." But for short-term, day-to-day comparisons, silver is much less liable to fluctuations and is still "the best measure of the altered value of things in a few years: because its vent is the same, and its quantity alters slowly."

63. In the mercantilist literature of the seventeenth century, this idea of proportional changes in money and price was often mistakenly thought to be an explanation of individual prices, so that if a commodity represented $\frac{1}{100}$ of all goods offered for sale, it would be worth $\frac{1}{100}$ of the money supply. Locke may have been answering this confusion, as well as illustrating how changes in the money supply can affect prices, in his example of the increase in the price of wheat. See Hegeland, p. 19.

64. *Some Considerations*, p. 78.

65. "That in a country where they had such a standing measure, any quantity of that money (if there were but so much that everybody might have some) would serve to drive any proportion of trade" (ibid., pp. 75–76).

66. Petty, 1:112–13.

67. *Some Considerations*, pp. 42–45.

68. Douglas Vickers interprets Locke's discussion as a description of income velocity (*Studies in the Theory of Money, 1690–1776*, p. 59). Arthur H. Leigh sees in Locke a clear discussion of the transactions demand for money ("John Locke and the Quantity Theory of Money," pp. 204–5).

69. *Some Considerations*, p. 38.

70. Ibid., pp. 41–42.

71. Remember that Locke was estimating the need for precious metals. If credit was a money substitute, less silver and gold would be necessary to "drive the trade."

72. *Some Considerations*, p. 39.

73. Ibid., pp. 39–40.

74. Ibid., p. 70.

75. Ibid., p. 62.

76. The concept of a circular flow is implicit, for example, in the

following passage: "The necessity of a certain proportion of money to trade, (I conceive) lies in this, that money in its circulation driving the several wheels of trade, whilst it keeps in that channel (for some of it will unavoidably be drained into standing pools) is shared between the landholder, whose land affords the materials; the labourer, who works them; the broker, i.e., merchant and shop-keeper, who distributes them to those that want them; and the consumer, who spends them" (ibid., pp. 30–31).

CHAPTER 3

1. Two economists in particular who classify Locke as a mercantilist are Eli F. Hecksher (*Mercantilism*) and Jacob Viner (*Studies in the Theory of International Trade,* pt. 1).

2. The major sources for this discussion of mercantilist economics are Hecksher, *Mercantilism,* 2:185–237; Viner, pp. 1–51; William D. Grampp, "The Liberal Elements in English Mercantilism," reprinted in Spengler and Allen, pp. 61–91; and Letwin, *Origins,* pt. 1. Both Hecksher and Viner believe that the advocacy of specie inflows was the major unifying element in the writings of the mercantilists, while Grampp finds their concern with full employment and economic growth of paramount importance. Letwin believes that their lack of a theoretical approach to economics was their most distinctive characteristic. Another useful source on mercantilism is Max Beer, *Early British Economics,* reprint ed., especially chaps. 6–10.

3. My summary of the "mercantilists" is not meant to imply that each and every writer in this group shared all the views which I attribute to them. In fact there was considerable variation in their arguments, which tended to increase in sophistication during the two centuries in which they wrote. However, in spite of the individual differences of opinion, there is a group of ideas that can be termed mercantilist doctrine during the time in which Locke published.

4. Specifically, although most mercantilists agreed that interest would fall as a result of increased money supply (Hecksher, p. 200), Locke was one of the first to assert that low interest did not necessarily mean prosperity. Among those who agreed with him on the latter point were Petty (who cannot be considered a mercantilist), John Pollexfen, and Thomas Manley. Dudley North had the

same idea at the same time as Locke, and John Law sometime afterward.

5. See Letwin, *Origins,* chap. 5; Hull's Introduction to Petty's *Economic Writings* (Petty, p. lxii); and Hecksher, *Mercantilism,* p. 183.

6. Petty, 1:244.

7. Letwin claims that Petty's methods bore no resemblance to mathematical statistics and that he was responsible only for giving statistics a name (*Origins,* p. 123). Schumpeter (pp. 210–11) agrees that Petty did not invent the science of statistics, but he quotes Davenport that Petty was the one who "brought it into rules and method."

8. Petty's "scientific approach" can easily be overemphasized. Although he was an enthusiastic supporter of the Baconian method, a member of the London experimental science group known as the Invisible College, and later a charter member of the Royal Society, like Locke's his interest stemmed from his medical background more than from his concern with economics. Although his economics does pay lip service to experimental techniques, his method is still deductive, as was Locke's.

9. Letwin, *Origins,* pp. 196–220.

10. Specifically, he disagreed with the views of Sir Josiah Child, who argued in his *Discourses about Trade* (1690) that the interest rate should be lowered to reduce the cost of production of goods. Child had originally published this argument in *Brief Observations Concerning Trade and Interest of Money* and *A Short Addition* in 1668, the year that Locke first began to write about economic questions. Child was not alone in his belief. It was shared by Culpepper, *A Discourse Shewing the Many Advantages Which Will Accrue in this Kingdom by the Abatement of Interest* (1668), and *The Necessity of Abating Interest Reasserted* (1670). Barbon also held this view to some extent. See Vickers, pp. 45–46.

11. Schumpeter points out (p. 106) that as far as moral attitudes are concerned, Protestant theologians in the sixteenth and seventeenth centuries continued to repeat Scholastic arguments both for and against interest-taking. For further analysis of this problem, see Bernard W. Dempsey, *Interest and Usury.*

12. The whole question of Locke's economic theories in the state of nature will be discussed in greater detail in chapter 4. The

following account of the effects of the origin of money is taken from the *Second Treatise*, chap. 5, especially pp. 317–18.

13. *Some Considerations*, p. 49.

14. Ibid., p. 56.

15. Ibid., p. 57.

16. One reason Locke may have had for comparing interest income to rental income was to provide his audience with an example close to their experience. Most of the MPs Locke wanted to convince were landowners who received some income from rents.

17. *Some Considerations*, p. 55. Notice the undoubtedly conscious and somewhat facetious echo of Aristotle's characterization of money as "barren."

18. *Some Considerations*, pp. 11, 19, 21.

19. Ibid., p. 33.

20. Ibid., pp. 42–43.

21. *Second Treatise*, p. 316.

22. Ibid., p. 306. See below, chapter 4, for further discussion of Locke's theory of property.

23. See below, p. 57, where he does indicate that borrowers will pay use "proportionably" to their want of money. This is hardly explicit enough, however, to be interpreted as a regular relationship between profit rates and interest rates.

24. Vickers (p. 51) states that Locke had no theory of capital but instead completely identified money and money capital. This interpretation is inescapable if the economic essays alone are taken into account, but if one examines the theories of the *Second Treatise*, Vickers's judgment is overly harsh. See also Hecksher, *Mercantilism*, 2:203; and Viner, p. 32.

25. Leigh, pp. 200–219, interprets Locke's theory of money in a more Keynesian light. He claims that when Locke says money has a double value (a value in use and a value in exchange), he was really adding the demand for money to hold as a function of the rate of interest to his transactions demand for money in the quantity equation. In this way, Leigh is able to integrate most of Locke's statements about money into a single theory. The weakness in this otherwise excellent article is that to support his argument, Leigh considers Locke's clearest statement of his quantity theory (*Some Considerations*, p. 71) to be a confusion of money as a stock vs. money as a flow. In fact, I believe it is this very passage which

provides the key to understanding Locke's theory of money and, indirectly, his theory of the value of goods. Here, *vent* is clearly Locke's term for the velocity of circulation, and there is no confusion between stocks and flows. See above, p. 42. See also Vickers, p. 57, where he emphasizes the separateness of Locke's analyses of interest and price levels, and suggests that this is characteristic of Locke's work as a whole.

26. *Some Considerations,* p. 2.

27. Ibid.

28. Ibid., p. 14.

29. Vickers (p. 47) disagrees with this conclusion, stating instead that Locke related interest only to the total supply of money in circulation and left the determinants of supply "virtually unanalyzed." He considers this passage to refer to a tendency to hoard money when interest rates are artificially depressed, with no purely theoretical significance as regards determinants of supply. I believe Vickers has missed the significance of Locke's description of men attempting to minimize risk when interest rates are low. Locke describes a situation wherein lenders lend less to high-risk producers when interest rates fall, clearly showing a direct relationship between price and quantity supplied. Furthermore, he gives a reason for this behavior—the return is too small given the risks of lending—implying that the proportion of risk to gain is one of the factors determining the quantity of funds supplied.

30. *Some Considerations,* p. 11.

31. Ibid., pp. 10–11.

32. Ibid., p. 6.

33. Ibid., pp. 102–3.

34. Ibid., p. 8.

35. It is interesting that Locke did not abandon the concept of a legal rate of interest after he preached with such vehemence against setting interest rates that were different from the natural rate. In fact, Locke never questioned that interest should be regulated, but only attempted to define how the regulation should be conducted. It was only because of this supposed monopoly of lenders, however, that a legal rate was necessary. He was not insensitive to the fact that there are administrative and legislative difficulties involved in setting up a legal rate of interest according to his criterion (see *Some Considerations,* pp. 103–4). He realized that if loanable funds were

concentrated in the hands of a monopoly, as he claimed was the case, it would be difficult to discern what the natural rate of interest actually was, and so he gave a rule of thumb: the interest rate should be set not so high that it would "eat up the merchant's and tradesman's profit" and not so low that it would "hinder men from risquing their money in other men's hands, and so rather choose to keep it out of trade." To arrive at this middle ground, he referred to the value of land to set the natural rate of interest. See below, pp. 60–61.

36. *Some Considerations,* pp. 2–3.

37. Ibid., p. 7.

38. Evidence of this mistrust can also be seen in Locke's argument against the Act to Regulate Printing of 1694, where he contended that the monopoly it would give to printers was "uneconomic" and contrary to the public interest. For excerpts of Locke's opinion of the consequences of the act, see Fox-Bourne, pp. 312–15; and for an evaluation of the opinion, see Cranston, *John Locke,* pp. 386–87.

39. See Soudek, p. 64.

40. *Some Considerations,* p. 11.

41. Ibid., p. 102.

42. Ibid., p. 2.

43. Ibid., p. 11.

44. Ibid., pp. 2–3.

45. Ibid., pp. 6–9.

46. Ibid., p. 12.

47. Ibid., p. 13. Letwin (*Origins,* p. 169) quotes this passage as an example of Locke's ability to cut through all the "rhetoric of superstition" about the benefits from lowering interest rates and to distinguish between the good of a private individual (a merchant or a usurer) and the general good—a distinction not difficult in itself, yet one that was "unusually clear-minded" given the beliefs of his contemporaries.

48. *Some Considerations,* p. 13.

49. Ibid., p. 14.

50. Ibid., p. 107.

51. Vickers, p. 47.

52. See above, chap. 3, n. 4.

53. In fact, Locke claimed that the existing six per cent rate of

interest was a disequilibrium rate which contributed to the existing monopoly of funds in bankers' hands and was causing a shortage of loanable funds on high risk loans (*Some Considerations*, pp. 6 and 125).

54. Hecksher, *Mercantilism*, 2:204.

55. *Some Considerations*, p. 32.

56. Ibid., pp. 48–49.

57. Ibid., p. 49. Locke's insistence that there is no connection between changes in the rate of interest and the price except insofar as a change in the rate of interest may alter the quantity of money or commodities in circulation further undermines Leigh's interpretation of Locke's theory of money. See above, chap. 3, n. 25.

58. *Some Considerations*, p. 14.

59. Ibid., p. 77.

60. Ibid., pp. 78–79.

61. Ibid., p. 79.

62. Viner (pp. 76–78) also agrees that Locke did not have any kind of price-specie-flow mechanism, although he does credit Locke with advancing the theory of international trade beyond what it had been until his time. Viner, however, is too harsh when he says that all Locke had of the self-regulating mechanism "was the quantity theory of money, and even here at the critical point he failed to make use of it and implied instead that a serious maladjustment between prices and the quantity of money was likely to be corrected, presumably permanently, by a consequent change in the volume of trade as by a change in prices." As I hypothesize below, England's trade position may have been such that Locke's analysis was the correct one after all.

63. Again, this is consistent with an assumption of inelastic demand for British exports.

64. Thomas Mun, *England's Treasure by Forraign Trade*, p. 128.

65. *Some Considerations*, pp. 26–29.

66. Hecksher (*Mercantilism*, 2:195) provides a partial list of mercantilists who desired the accumulation of precious metals for its own sake rather than as a means to increase consumption. It includes such illustrious names as Mun, Petty, and Davenant.

67. *Some Considerations*, p. 14.

68. Ibid., p. 15.

69. Hecksher, *Mercantilism*, 2:191 ff.

70. *Some Considerations,* pp. 26–28. This analogy was common in mercantilist literature. It appears in the writings of John Hales (1581), Misselden (1622), Mun (1664), and Samuel Lamb (1659), among others. See Viner, pp. 32–33.

71. Although Locke does not say this directly, it can be inferred from the structure of his argument. First he describes how a country can achieve an inflow of precious metals by maintaining a favorable balance of trade (pp. 24–29). Then (pp. 29–30) he follows this up by saying, "We have seen how riches and money are got, kept, or lost, in any country. . . . The next thing to be considered is, how money is necessary to trade." He goes on to analyze how much money is needed to drive the trade, implying that this is the reason for a country to try to accumulate metals in the first place.

72. Viner, pp. 76–78.

73. *Some Considerations,* pp. 77–78.

74. This was a common mercantilist belief, although it was not backed up by theoretical analysis as was Locke's. See Hecksher, "Mercantilism," *Economic History Review* 7 (November 1936): 48.

75. Viner (p. 79) believes that the specie points must have been recognized by merchants as soon as they started engaging in trade, and he finds an "adequate" statement of such recognition by Gresham in 1558. Locke probably understood the mechanism as a result of his personal observation of exchange rates over the course of his lifetime. His personal diaries are full of notes on the weight and fineness of foreign coins and the fluctuations in the rate of exchange. These notes are most prevalent during the years he spent in France and the years he was in hiding in Holland.

76. *Some Considerations,* p. 117.

77. Ibid., pp. 117–18.

78. Wu Chi-yuen (*An Outline of International Price Theories,* p. 50) also notes Locke's items in the balance of payments and considers the treatment an advancement over Mun's.

79. *Some Considerations,* p. 19.

80. Ibid.

81. Ibid., p. 20.

82. Cf. *Second Treatise,* chap. 5.

83. "The landholder. . .is the person, that bearing the greatest part of the burdens of The Kingdom, ought, I think, to have the greatest care taken of him" (*Some Considerations,* p. 100).

84. Ibid., pp. 55–56.

85. Ibid., p. 57.

86. Ibid., p. 58.

87. Ibid., p. 52. It is interesting that North made the same argument in his *Discourses,* p. 4.

88. *Some Considerations,* pp. 59–60.

89. Ibid., p. 60.

90. Ibid. Peter Laslett (*The World We Have Lost*) remarks that in the seventeenth century, it was assumed that any man who made money in trade would immediately want to acquire that most English of dreams, a place in the country. Hence Locke's belief that when trade was thriving, the demand for land would be correspondingly high, and vice versa.

91. *Some Considerations,* p. 100.

92. Ibid., p. 101.

93. Grampp (pp. 61–91) believes that unemployment was one of the primary mercantilist concerns, occasioning many of their policy recommendations on interest and foreign trade: "the unemployment of the sixteenth and seventeenth centuries was the result of immobility, of seasonal fluctuations, of the rigidity of certain prices and wages which was produced by the monopolistic practises of the guilds, and of the frequent and severe deflations." Among the historical events that were responsible we could add the enclosure movement, the Cromwell rebellion, the resulting political uncertainty until the reign of William and Mary, and the Dutch wars.

CHAPTER 4

1. "To understand Political Power right, and derive it from its Original, we must consider what State all Men are naturally in, and that is, a *State of perfect Freedom* to order their Actions, and dispose of their Possessions, and Persons as they think fit, within the bounds of the Law of Nature, without asking leave, or depending upon the Will of any other Man" (*Second Treatise,* p. 287).

2. Although there has been much discussion in recent years as to whether or not Locke did, in fact, believe in natural law, we will take him at his word in the *Second Treatise.* Most of those who argue against such a position rest their case on the fact that Locke promised to construct the content of the law of nature several times during his lifetime but never followed through on his promise.

This, his critics say, is proof that he ceased to believe in such a law at some time but refused to admit it publicly; but it is equally possible that during his publishing years he was so busy with his political interests, and during his retirement with his commentaries on the scriptures, that he just did not have time to work on such a difficult problem. Or it could very well be, as John Dunn has recently suggested in *The Political Thought of John Locke,* that the task itself is impossible. Whatever the reason, I will take it as a given that Locke most certainly did believe in the existence of a natural moral law, discoverable through men's reason, at least when he wrote the *Two Treatises* and his economic essays. For further discussion of Locke's tentative natural law theory, see Dunn, *Political Thought,* pp. 187–99; and Von Leyden, ed., *Essays.* Some exponents of the theory that Locke did not have a natural law theory are: Willmoore Kendall (*John Locke and the Doctrine of Majority Rule*); Leo Strauss (*Natural Right and History*); and C. B. MacPherson (*The Political Theory of Possessive Individualism: Hobbes to Locke*). Those who do attribute a natural law theory to Locke include J. W. Gough (*The Social Contract,* 2d ed. rev.; and *John Locke's Political Philosophy*); Laslett, in the introduction to his edition of the *Two Treatises;* Sterling Lamprecht (*Moral and Political Philosophy of John Locke*); Martin Seliger (*The Liberal Politics of John Locke*); and Dunn (*Political Thought*).

3. *Second Treatise,* p. 289.

4. Ibid.

5. Ibid., p. 294.

6. Ibid., p. 368.

7. Ibid., p. 304.

8. For a discussion which contrasts Locke's view of original ownership with Grotius's and Pufendorf's, see Seliger, pp. 180–85.

9. *Second Treatise,* p. 304.

10. Ibid., p. 306.

11. Ibid., pp. 305–6.

12. Ibid., p. 307.

13. Ibid., p. 306.

14. Specifically, Pascal Larkin, *Property in the Eighteenth Century with Special Reference to England and John Locke,* p. 67; and Gough, *John Locke's Political Philosophy,* p. 82.

15. *Second Treatise,* p. 307.

16. *Second Treatise,* p. 340.

17. The idea of servants' existing in the state of nature is too much for some of Locke's critics to take seriously. MacPherson (p. 216) states that the evidence that Locke included servants in the state of nature would be acceptable, "were it not that the idea of wage-labor in a state of nature seems too patent an absurdity to attribute to Locke," although he agrees that this is exactly what must be attributed to him given his arguments. Gough (*John Locke's Political Philosophy,* p. 92) finds the inclusion of wage labor makes Locke's state of nature "more incredible than ever. . . . Did he really think that a sophisticated commercial economy could exist without political government, in the state of nature?" Laslett (*Two Treatises,* p. 104n.) believes that "though he seems specific enough. . .in making the master own his servants' labour, it is not clearly a matter of wage relationship." J. E. Parsons, Jr. ("Locke's Doctrine of Property," p. 402) says that while Locke suggests that a servant's labor is the property of the master, "yet in the state of nature very few men can be presumed to have had servants." Given Locke's doctrine, I can see nothing absurd or incredible in his putting wage labor in the state of nature. For a state of nature to obtain, all that is necessary is that there be no formal ruling authority; this does not preclude the existence of family relationships, including the practice of taking a stranger into the family to act as a paid servant. Laslett (*The World We Have Lost*) has pointed out that in seventeenth-century England it was very common for even poor households to have a servant or two, usually an adolescent child of even poorer parentage who would remain as part of the family until it was time for him (or her) to marry and set up his own household. Perhaps MacPherson (p. 197) is correct that Locke "read back into the state of nature certain preconceptions about the nature of seventeenth-century man and society" when he postulated the existence of servants and wage labor even in relatively poor conditions. Yet the idea itself is not ridiculous, especially when it is remembered that the state of nature was as much an analytic as a historic concept. It should be noted that from the context of the passage it is clear that the servants were cutting turfs on the common—therefore in civil society and not the state of nature. Still, Locke was using the common as a way of illustrating a principle that began in the state of nature and continued into civil society. Hence,

it is reasonable to conclude that Locke did believe that servants—
and therefore wage labor—existed in the state of nature.

18. *Second Treatise,* p. 308.

19. Ibid., p. 314.

20. For example, Hannah Robie Sewall, *The Theory of Value
before Adam Smith,* American Economic Association Publications,
ser. 3, no. 2 (1901), p. 75; and Spiegel, *Growth,* p. 164.

21. *Second Treatise,* p. 314.

22. Locke also makes the astute observation that private property
is beneficial to society because it increases the common stock available for others to use: "he, that encloses land and has a greater
plenty of the conveniences of life from ten acres, than he could have
from a hundred left to nature, may truly be said, to give ninety
acres to mankind" (ibid.).

23. Ibid., p. 315.

24. Ibid.

25. Ibid.

26. Ibid., p. 316.

27. See Vaughn, "John Locke and the Labor Theory of Value,"
*Journal of Libertarian Studies,* vol. 2, no. 4 (winter, 1978).

28. *Second Treatise,* p. 315.

29. Ibid., p. 317.

30. Harrison and Laslett, pp. 207–8.

31. *Second Treatise,* p. 314.

32. Petty, 1:68.

33. Petty, 1:181. *The Political Anatomy of Ireland,* although
written in 1671, was not published until 1691. Locke apparently
did not own a copy of the book.

34. *Second Treatise,* pp. 315, 317.

35. Ibid., p. 308.

36. Ibid.

37. Ibid., p. 309.

38. Ibid., pp. 313, 317.

39. Ibid., p. 319.

40. Ibid., p. 308. See also p. 314: "we see how labor could make
men distinct titles to several parcels of it [the world], for their
private uses; wherein there could be no doubt of right, no room for
quarrel"; and p. 320, where he again reiterates that before money
came into use, "right and conveniency went together. . . . This left

no room for controversy about the title, nor for incroachment on the right of others; what portion a man carved to himself, was easily seen; and it was useless as well as dishonest to carve himself too much, or take more than he needed.''

41. Ibid., pp. 318–19.

42. Locke's strange use of the word *consent* to describe the evolution of some man-made institution might best be understood as an example of what Hayek meant by an institution which arises from human action, but not by human design, that is, an institution that arises as a manifestation of a spontaneous order in society. See Friedrich Hayek, *Studies in Philosophy, Politics and Economics,* p. 96.

43. Locke describes the process by which barter eventually leads to the identification of a money-commodity and concludes that if a person ''would give his nuts for a piece of metal, pleased with its color; or exchange his sheep for shells, or wool for a sparkling pebble or diamond, and keep those by him all his life, he invaded not the right of others, he might heap up as much of these durable things as he pleased; the exceeding of the bounds of his just property not lying in the largness of his possession, but the perishing of anything uselessly in it'' (*Second Treatise,* pp. 318–19).

44. ''And as different degrees of industry were apt to give men possessions in different proportions, so this *invention of money* gave them the opportunity to continue and enlarge them''; and ''Find out something that hath the *use and value of money* amongst his neighbors, you shall see the same man will begin presently to *enlarge* his *possessions''* (ibid., p. 319).

Seliger (pp. 154–55) also points out that men had unequal property before the introduction of money. Money simply enabled men to increase the inequality of possessions.

45. See for example *Second Treatise,* pp. 368–71. In addition to the explicit economic motive for establishing government, Locke also claims men have a ''love, and want of society,'' which brings them together and induces them to leave the state of nature. See p. 352 and especially pp. 336–37. Despite these passages, however, Locke's emphasis throughout the *Second Treatise* is on the ''inconveniences'' and ''insecurities'' of the state of nature, which cause men to unite under a civil government.

46. ''In some parts of the world, (where the increase of people

and stock, with the use of money) had made land scarce, and so of some value, the several communities settled the bounds of their distinct territories'' (ibid., p. 317; see also p. 313).

47. Ibid., p. 368.

48. Ibid., Laslett's Introduction, p. 101.

49. Ibid., pp. 371, 378. See also p. 370: "But though men when they enter into society, give up the equality, liberty, and executive power they had in the state of nature, into the hands of the society, to be so far disposed of by the legislative, as the good of the society shall require; yet it [is] only with an intention in every one the better to preserve himself his liberty and property"; and p. 378: "For the preservation of property being the end of government, and that for which men enter into society, it necessarily supposes and requires, that the people should have property, without which they must be supposed to lose that by entering into society, which was the end for which they entered into it, too gross an absurdity for any man to own."

50. Ibid., p. 424.

51. Ibid., p. 367.

52. Ibid., p. 424.

53. Ibid., p. 366.

54. Ibid., p. 367. That is, he could not declare his land a separate country and cut himself off from the rest of society. His land was part of the commonwealth.

55. *John Locke and the Doctrine of Majority Rule;* and "John Locke Revisited," pp. 217–34.

56. Kendall, *John Locke,* p. 71.

57. *Some Considerations,* pp. 62, 100–101. This will be explored in greater detail in the next chapter.

58. *Second Treatise,* pp. 382–92.

59. Ibid., p. 430.

60. Ibid., pp. 430–31.

61. Ibid., p. 429.

62. MacPherson, pp. 194–262.

63. *Second Treatise,* p. 199.

64. Ibid., p. 308.

65. Ibid., pp. 201–2.

66. Ibid., p. 207.

67. Ibid.

68. Bod. L. MSS. Locke, C. 30, fol. 18. The notes continue:

Trade is two fold. 1° Domestic manufacture whereby is to be understood all labor employed by your people in preparing commodities for your consumption either of your own people (where it will exclude importation) or of foraigners. 2° Cariage i.e., navigacion & merchandise. People also are two fold. 1° Those that contribute any way to your trade, especially in commodities for exportation, the chief whereof are men employed in Husbandry. Drapory and mines and navigacion. 2° Such as are either idle and so do not help as Retainers to Gentry and beggars or which is worse, hinder trade as retailers in some degree, multitudes of lawyers but above all, soldiers in pay.
Promoters of traders:
 Freedom of traders
 Naturalization easy
 Freedom of religion
 Register of certainty of property
 Small customs
 Publique workhouses
 Coin good certain hard to be counterfieted
 Transferring of bills
 Increase and encouragement of seamen in an Island not
  seamen nor navigacion in a continent that wants not
  supplys but can subsist of itself
 Cheap labor
 Fashions suited to your own manufacture
 Suitable manufacturers to your markets whose commod-
  ities are want
 Low customs on exportations
 New manufactures at home
Hindrance of trade:
 Intricacy of law
 Arests
 Arbitrary power
 Vices tending to prodigality

69. Kelly (p. 223) believes that these notes may have been intended to form the basis for a speech or short pamphlet on trade while Locke was secretary to the Council for Trade and Plantations.

70. See *Some Considerations*, pp. 19–20.

71. MacPherson, p. 212.

72. Here is an excellent example of MacPherson's value preconceptions interfering with his analyses. MacPherson argues that the
right to make a living through the use of one's own labor is not
equivalent to the right to own property because the propertyless
man must necessarily be dependent on the property-owner for his
livelihood. Hence, he says, Locke believed in a natural class distinction between those with property (the full citizens) and those
without (the inferior members of society). This interpretation is not
faithful to Locke's intention. Locke believed both that only the
industrious and rational would be able to acquire property and,
significantly, that only the industrious and rational would have the
ability to hold onto their property once they acquired it (see *Some
Considerations,* pp. 20, 72). If a man owned property but was lazy,
he would soon be forced to sell it to a more worthy person. There
was nothing to stop a wage earner from acquiring land with his
savings if he desired. Ownership of land was not confined to a
hereditary descent.

In addition, property did not consist only of land. It also consisted of goods and money which can be gotten through trade,
manufacture, and labor. Once men began to work the land, it
became possible for other kinds of enterprises to be engaged in and
more people could potentially become wealthy.

73. *Second Treatise,* p. 312.

74. MacPherson, p. 212.

75. Ibid., p. 209.

76. Ibid., p. 216.

77. Ibid., pp. 209–10.

78. Ibid., p. 220.

79. It is probably true that Locke believed that a class system was
natural to society, but it was one based on virtue and ability which
allowed for considerable mobility.

80. I am using capitalism here to mean a system of private
property ownership where property rights may be freely traded in
the market place. I assume that this is also MacPherson's definition.

## CHAPTER 5

1. Letwin, *Origins,* pp. 191–92. Bowley ("Some Seventeenth
Century Contributions," p. 132) also notes Locke's (and Barbon's)
contributions to scientific economics: "The deliberate setting out

and demonstration of the nature of exchange value, and of the nature of the factors affecting demand, as a necessary preliminary to the investigation of problems of economic policy must, I think, be regarded as a major contribution to the development of scientific economic analysis independent of any incidental originality in the expositions.''

2. Schumpeter, pp. 116–18.

3. Ibid., p. 116.

4. Ibid., pp. 117–18.

5. See, for example, Frederick Copleston, *A History of Philosophy*, vol. 5, pt. 1, p. 139; and Laslett's Introduction, *Two Treatises*, p. 86.

6. Hugo Grotius, *De Jure Belli Ac Pacis Libri Tres*.

7. Beer (p. 128) has noted the connection between Locke's economics and scholasticism, although in a manner unflattering to Locke. See also Kelly.

8. Schumpeter, p. 117.

9. *Second Treatise*, p. 320.

10. See above, p. 98.

11. *Second Treatise*, p. 342.

12. Ibid., p. 430.

13. See Letwin, *Origins*, pp. 156–99, and above, chap. 2.

14. *Some Considerations*, p. 102.

15. Ibid., pp. 46–68.

16. Ibid., pp. 2–3. Kelly also notes Locke's implicit assumption of rational economic self-interest throughout the economic essays.

17. Schumpeter (p. 99) credits de Lugo with interpreting Saint Thomas's conception of ''prudent economic reason'' to mean ''the intention of gaining in every legitimate way,'' although he did not intend this to constitute an approval of profit-hunting.

18. *Some Considerations*, pp. 2–3.

19. Not only does Locke objectively describe the consequences of economic self-interest to the functioning of the economy, but he also states that ''people have a right to as much of their money as it is worth. More they cannot get!''

Kelly also notes that in the *Second Treatise* Locke imputes to men a ''desire of having more than men need,'' which generates economic activity above mere subsistence. Kelly points out that Locke vacillates between treating this desire as ''the highest manifestation of rationality" and referring to it as *"amor sceleratus habendi"* (an evil concupiscence).

20. See, for example, Locke's description of how usury laws may lead to increased perjury in the nation as people create false contracts to cover up lending at higher rates of interest (*Some Considerations,* pp. 3–6).

21. Ibid., p. 13.

22. Ibid., p. 12.

23. Ibid., p. 100.

24. This in part explains why some historians of economic thought have considered Locke to be a mercantilist; this, and the fact that Locke also seemed to be in favor of so many mercantilist policies, a favorable balance of trade, encouragement of manufacturing, distrust of middlemen, maintenance of a stable currency, and abundance of skilled labor to mention but a few.

25. Locke actually calls the current state of the money market a monopoly "by consent" since there was no official granting of monopoly privilege to any banker. The effective monopoly developed, however, because the legal price was held below the equilibrium price, causing people to concentrate their lending in less risky markets (*Some Considerations,* pp. 6–9, 103).

26. Ibid., p. 111.

27. *Second Treatise,* pp. 376–78.

28. Locke argued this with great force in *Further Considerations.*

29. *Second Treatise,* p. 380.

30. Locke's Poor Law Reforms are reprinted in Fox-Bourne, pp. 377–91.

31. Ibid., pp. 363–72. Letwin (*Origins*) also mentions Locke's recommendations on the Irish linen trade as evidence that Locke did not believe in a policy of laissez faire.

32. Letwin, *Origins,* p. 194.

33. In several instances, Locke does assert that it is the government's responsibility to look after foreign trade to assure that England does not grow poor through trade deficits. See, for instance, *Some Considerations,* p. 100, where he states that bringing in more wealth from abroad, "being the only concernment of the kingdom, in reference to its wealth, is apt to be supposed by us without doors to be the only care of a Parliament"; and later, on p. 115, where he suggests that losses of specie are the result of "the

mal-administration of neglected or mis-managed government.'' However, he is openly contemptuous of laws against export of specie and places the blame for trade deficits on more consumption of ''claret, spice, silk, and other foreign consumable wares, than our exportation of commodities does exchange for'' (*Some Considerations*, p. 116). The remedy he seems to suggest is more frugality on the part of wealthy ''landed gentlemen'' and a government that does not make matters worse through following ill-advised interest policies and allowing the coinage to deteriorate.

34. Letwin, *Origins*, p. 193.

35. *Some Considerations*, p. 102.

36. *Political Studies*, pp. 68–87. *Venditio* is found on pp. 84–87. It is also reprinted in Kelly.

37. *Venditio*, in Dunn, ''Locke's Political Theory,'' p. 84. Locke's identification of the market price at the place of sale as the just price is very much a scholastic idea. It was found in the writings of Thomas Aquinas, Bernardino of Siena, Cardinal Cajetan, and Francisco de Vitoria, to name but a few. It was also borrowed by the Puritan theologian Richard Baxter (De Roover, ''Just Price,'' pp. 9–21). John W. Baldwin (''The Medieval Theories of the Just Price'') agrees with this interpretation of Aquinas's view of the just price and adds to the list Giles of Lessines, Henry of Ghent, Richard of Middletown, Jean Buridan, and Antonius of Florence (pp. 75–76).

38. *Venditio*, in Dunn, ''Locke's Political Theory,'' p. 84.

39. Ibid., pp. 84–85.

40. Ibid., p. 85.

41. Notice also that Locke here calls this intrinsic value the ''natural'' value of a good. This is a change from *Some Considerations* where natural value referred to the market price, and it is interesting to speculate why he might have changed his terminology here. One possibility might be that in between the publication of *Some Considerations* and the writing of *Venditio*, Locke reread Petty's *Treatise of Taxes and Contributions* and adopted his terminology.

42. Again, this is also the medieval reason for believing that the market price is the just price.

43. *Venditio*, in Dunn, ''Locke's Political Theory,'' p. 85.

44. De Roover (''Just Price,'' pp. 15–16) notes that all forms of

price discrimination were condemned by the Scholastics, including Aquinas, Duns Scotus, and Bernardino of Siena. See also Baldwin, pp. 79–80.

45. *Venditio,* in Dunn, "Locke's Political Theory," pp. 85–87.

46. Ibid., pp. 85–86.

47. Ibid., p. 86.

48. Dunn considers the above passage as evidence that the central problem of *Venditio* is Locke's attempt to reconcile the basically contradictory virtues of justice and charity.

49. "For the buyer not knowing what the commodity cost the merchant to purchase and bring thither could be under no tie of giving him the profit of 5–10 per cent" (ibid., p. 86); and "The price which the anchor cost him which is the market price at another place makes no part of the price which he fairly sells it for at sea" (ibid., p. 87; this is in reference to a situation where one ship wants to purchase another ship's anchor at sea).

50. Ibid., p. 87.

51. Ibid.

52. Cf. *Some Considerations,* p. 51.

53. In fact, as mentioned above, in *Some Considerations* Locke definitely believes that there are times when the harmony of interests does not prevail, when instead the interests of some parts of the economy are exactly the opposite of the interests of society as a whole. This is true of merchants as a group since "the merchant may get by a trade that makes the kingdom poor" (p. 87), although he fails to specify what kind of trade he is referring to, and it is especially true of "brokers," or middlemen, who "hinder. . . the trade of any country, by making the circuit which the money goes, larger, and in the circuit more stops, so that the returns must necessarily be slower and scantier, to the prejudice of trade." Locke apparently believes there to be a coincidence of the interests of landholder, laborers, and manufacturers, but he does not believe the same about people who make their living by selling what has already been produced. This attitude was, of course, common into the nineteenth century.

CHAPTER 6

1. Letwin, *Origins,* pp. 158–95.

2. Letwin, *Origins,* p. 187.

# BIBLIOGRAPHY

PRIMARY SOURCES

Aristotle. *Politics*. Translated by J. A. Sinclair. Baltimore: Penguin Books, 1962.

Aristotle. *Ethics*. Translated by J. A. K. Thomson. Baltimore: Penguin Books, 1953.

Barbon, Nicholas. *A Discourse of Trade*. 1690. Hollander Reprint, 1905.

Grotius, Hugo. *De Jure Belli Ac Pacis Libri Tres*. Edited by James Brown Scott. 2 vols. Oxford: Clarendon Press, 1925.

Laslett, Peter, and John Harrison. *The Library of John Locke*, Oxford Bibliographical Society Publications, n.s., vol. 13. Oxford: Oxford University Press, 1965.

Locke, John. *An Essay Concerning Human Understanding*. Edited by Alexander Campbell Fraser. 2 vols. New York: Dover, 1959.

————. *Essays on the Law of Nature*. Edited by W. von Leyden. Oxford: Clarendon Press, 1954.

————. *Two Treatises of Government*. Edited by Peter Laslett. 2d ed. Cambridge: Cambridge University Press, 1953.

————. *Several Papers Relating to Money, Interest and Trade, etcetera*. 1696. Reprint ed., New York: Augustus M. Kelley, 1968.

Long, P. *A Summary Catalogue of the Lovelace Collection of the Papers of John Locke in the Bodleian Library*, Oxford Bibliographical Society Publications, n.s., vol. 13. Oxford: Oxford University Press, 1956.

Marx, Karl. *Capital.* Edited by Frederick Engels. Translated by Samuel Moore and Edward Aveling. New York: Modern Library, 1906.

———. *Theories of Surplus Value.* Translated by G. A. Bonner and Emile Burns. New York: International Publishers, 1952.

Mun, Thomas, *England's Treasure by Forraign Trade.* 1664. Reprint ed., Cambridge, 1954.

McCulloch, John R., ed. *A Selected Collection of Scarce and Valuable Tracts on Money.* 1856. Reprint ed., New York: Augustus M. Kelley, 1966.

———. *Early English Tracts on Commerce.* 1859. Reprint ed., Cambridge: Cambridge University Press, 1954.

North, Dudley. *A Discourse of Trade.* 1690. Hollander Reprint, 1905.

Petty, Sir William. *Economic Writings of Sir William Petty.* Edited by C. H. Hull. 2 vols. Cambridge: Cambridge University Press, 1899.

Pufendorf, Samuel. *De Jure Naturae et Gentium.* Trans. C. H. and W. A. Oldfather. Vol. 2. Oxford: Clarendon Press, 1934.

Smith, Adam. *The Wealth of Nations.* Edited by Edwin Cannan. New York: Random House, 1937.

### BIOGRAPHY

Aaron, R. I. *John Locke.* London: Oxford University Press, 1937.

Brown, Louise Fargo. *The First Earl of Shaftesbury.* New York: Appleton-Century, 1933.

Cranston, Maurice. *Locke.* London: Longmans, Green, 1961.

———. *John Locke: A Biography.* New York: Macmillan, 1957.

Dewhurst, Kenneth. *John Locke: Physician and Philosopher.* London: Wellcome Historical Medical Library, 1963.

Fox-Bourne, H. R. *The Life of John Locke.* 2 vols. New York: Harper, 1876.

King, Peter (seventh Lord King). *The Life and Letters of John Locke.* London: George Bell and Sons, 1884.

More, Louis Trenchard. *The Life and Works of the Honourable Robert Boyle.* New York: Oxford University Press, 1944.

# Bibliography

SECONDARY SOURCES

Beer, Max. *Early British Economics.* 1938. Reprint ed., New York: Augustus M. Kelley, 1967.

Bonar, James. *Philosophy and Political Economy.* 3rd ed. rev. London: George Allen and Unwin, 1922.

Bowley, Marian. *Studies in the History of Economic Theory before 1870.* London: MacMillan, 1973.

Butterfield, Herbert. *The Origins of Modern Science, 1300-1800.* Rev. ed. New York: Collier Books, 1962.

Carleton, John D. *Westminster School: A History.* London: Rupert Hart-Davis, 1965.

Clapham, Sir John. *A Concise Economic History of Britain.* Cambridge: Cambridge University Press, 1949.

Clark, Sir George. *The Seventeenth Century.* New York: Galaxy Books, 1961.

Copleston, Frederick. *A History of Philosophy.* 8 vols. Vols. 4, 5, and 6. Garden City, N.Y.: Image Books, 1964.

Crombie, A. C. *Medieval and Early Modern Science.* 2d ed. rev. 2 vols. Vol. 2. Garden City, N.Y.: Anchor Books, 1959.

Czajkoroski, Casimir J. *The Theory of Private Property in John Locke's Political Philosophy.* Notre Dame, Ind.: Edwards Brothers, 1941.

Dempsey, Bernard W. *Interest and Usury.* Washington, D.C.: American Council on Public Affairs, 1943.

Dunn, John. *The Political Thought of John Locke.* Cambridge: Cambridge University Press, 1969.

Fraser, Campbell. *John Locke as a Factor in Modern Thought.* Proceedings of the British Academy, Vol. 1. October 28, 1904.

Gough, J. W. *John Locke's Political Philosophy.* 2d ed. Oxford: Clarendon Press, 1950.

————. *The Social Contract.* 2d ed. rev. Oxford: Clarendon Press, 1957.

Grice-Hutchinson, Marjorie. *The School of Salamanca: Readings in Spanish Monetary Theory, 1544-1605.* Oxford: Clarendon Press, 1952.

Hall, Marie Boas. *Robert Boyle on Natural Philosophy.* Bloomington, Ind.: Indiana University Press, 1965.

————. *Robert Boyle and Seventeenth Century Chemistry.* Cambridge: Cambridge University Press, 1965.

Hayek, Friedrich. *Studies in Philosophy, Politics and Economics.* Chicago: University of Chicago Press, 1967.

Heaton, Herbert. *Economic History of Europe.* Rev. ed. New York: Harper and Row, 1948.

Hecksher, Eli F. *Mercantilism.* Translated by Mendel Shapiro. 2 vols. London: Allen and Unwin, 1935.

Hegeland, Hugo. *The Quantity Theory of Money.* Goteborg: Elanders Boktryckeri Aktiebolag, 1951.

Johnson, E. A. H. *Predecessors of Adam Smith.* 1937. Reprint ed., New York: Augustus M. Kelley, 1965.

Kelly, Patrick, Hyde, ed. *Locke on Money.* Manuscript.

Kendall, Willmoore. *John Locke and the Doctrine of Majority Rule.* 1941. Reprint ed., Urbana: University of Illinois Press, 1959.

Keynes, John Maynard. *The General Theory of Employment, Interest, and Money.* 1936. Reprint ed., New York: Harcourt, Brace, and World, 1964.

Kraus, John L. *John Locke: Empiricist, Atomist, Conceptualist and Agnostic.* New York: Philosophical Library, 1968.

Lamprecht, Sterling. *Moral and Political Philosophy of John Locke.* New York: Columbia University Press, 1918.

Laslett, Peter. *The World We Have Lost.* New York: Scribner, 1965.

Larkin, Pascal. *Property in the Eighteenth Century with Special Reference to England and John Locke.* Cork: Cork University Press, 1930.

Letwin, William. *The Origins of Scientific Economics.* Garden City, N.Y.: Anchor Books, 1965.

————. *Sir Josiah Child: Merchant Economist.* Kress Library of Business and Economics, no. 14. Cambridge: Harvard University Printing Office, 1959.

MacPherson, C. B. *The Political Theory of Possessive Individualism: Hobbes to Locke.* Oxford: Clarendon Press, 1962.

Mallet, Charles Edward. *A History of the University of Oxford.* 3 vols. Vol. 2. London: Methuen, 1924.

Meek, Ronald L. *Studies in the Labour Theory of Value.* London: Lawrence and Wishart, 1956.

# Bibliography

Monroe, Arthur Eli. *Monetary Theory before Adam Smith.* Harvard Economic Studies, vol. 25. Cambridge: Harvard University Press, 1923.

———. *Early Economic Thought.* Cambridge: Harvard University Press, 1924.

O'Conner, D. J. *John Locke.* Rev. ed. New York: Dover, 1967.

Ogg, David. *England in the Reigns of James II and William III.* Oxford: Clarendon Press, 1955.

Purver, Margery. *The Royal Society: Concept and Creation.* Cambridge, Mass.: MIT Press, 1967.

Rich, E. E., and C. H. Welson, eds. *The Cambridge Economic History of Europe.* 2d ed. Vol. 4. Cambridge: Cambridge University Press, 1967.

Roll, Eric. *A History of Economic Thought.* 3d ed. Englewood Cliffs, N.J.: Prentice-Hall, 1953.

Sabine, George H. *A History of Political Theory.* Rev. ed. New York: Holt, Rinehart and Winston, 1950.

Schumpeter, Joseph A. *History of Economic Analysis.* New York: Oxford University Press, 1954.

Seliger, Martin. *The Liberal Politics of John Locke.* New York: Praeger, 1969.

*A Short History of Science: A Symposium.* Garden City, N.Y.: Doubleday Anchor, 1952.

Spiegel, Henry W., ed. *The Development of Economic Thought.* New York: John Wiley, 1964.

———. *The Growth of Economic Thought.* Englewood Cliffs, N.J.: Prentice-Hall, 1971.

Stark, Werner. *The Ideal Foundations of Economic Thought.* New York: Oxford University Press, 1944.

Strauss, Leo. *Natural Right and History.* Chicago: University of Chicago Press, 1953.

Vickers, Douglas. *Studies in the Theory of Money, 1690–1776.* Philadelphia: Chilton, 1959.

Viner, Jacob. *Studies in the Theory of International Trade.* 1937. Reprint ed., New York: Augustus M. Kelley, 1965.

Willey, Basil. *The Seventeenth Century Background.* 1935. Reprint ed., Garden City, N.Y.: Doubleday Anchor, 1953.

Wu Chi-yuen. *An Outline of International Price Theories.* London:

# Bibliography

George Routledge and Sons, 1939.

Yolton, John W., ed. *John Locke: Problems and Perspectives.* Cambridge: Cambridge University Press, 1969.

ARTICLES

Anderson, Fulton H. "The Influence of Contemporary Science on Locke's Method and Results." *University of Toronto Studies: Philosophy,* vol. 2 (1923): 3–31.

Baldwin, John W. "The Medieval Theories of the Just Price: Romanists, Canonists, and Theologians in the Twelfth and Thirteenth Centuries." *Transactions of the American Philosophical Society,* n.s., vol. 49, no. 4 (1959). Reprinted in *Pre-Capitalist Economic Thought: Three Modern Interpretations,* pp. 3–92. New York: Arno Press, 1972.

Bowley, Marian. "Some Seventeenth Century Contributions to the Theory of Value." *Economica,* n.s., vol. 30 (1963): 122–39.

Chalk, Alfred F. "Natural Law and the Rise of Economic Individualism in England." *Journal of Political Economy* 59 (June 1951): 332–47.

Dempsey, Bernard W. "Just Price in a Functional Economy." *American Economic Review* 25 (September 1935): 471–86. Reprinted in *Essays in Economic Thought: Aristotle to Marshall,* ed. J. J. Spengler and W. R. Allen, pp. 45–60. Chicago: Rand McNally, 1960.

De Roover, Raymond. "The Concept of the Just Price: Theory and Economic Policy." *Journal of Economic History* 18 (December 1958): 9–21. Reprinted in *Readings in the History of Economic Theory,* ed. Ingrid H. Rima, pp. 9–21. New York: Holt, Rinehart and Winston, 1970.

———. "Monopoly Theory Prior to Adam Smith." *Quarterly Journal of Economics* 65 (November 1951): 492–524.

Dunn, John. "Justice and Locke's Political Theory," *Political Studies* 16 (1968): 68–87.

Holtrop, M. W. "Theories of the Velocity of Circulation of Money in Early Economic Literature." *Economic History* 1 (January 1929): 503–24.

Hundert, E. J. "Market Society and Meaning in Locke's Political Philosophy." *Journal of the History of Philosophy* 15 (1977): 33–44.

172

# Bibliography

Kendall, Willmoore. "John Locke Revisited." *Intercollegiate Review* 2 (January/February 1966): 217–34.

Kirzner, Israel. "Producer, Entrepreneur and the Right to Property." *Reason Papers,* no. 1 (fall, 1974).

Laslett, Peter. "John Locke, the Great Recoinage, and the Origins of the Board of Trade, 1695-1698." *William and Mary Quarterly* 14 (July 1957): 370–92.

Leigh, Arthur H. "John Locke and the Quantity Theory of Money." *History of Political Economy* 6 (summer, 1974): 200–219.

Lowry, S. Todd. "Aristotle's Mathematical Analysis of Exchange." *History of Political Economy* 1 (spring, 1969): 44–66.

Muchmore, Lynn. "Gerard de Malynes and Mercantile Economics." *History of Political Economy* 1 (fall, 1969): 336–58.

Parsons, J. E., Jr. "Locke's Doctrine of Property." *Social Research* 36 (autumn, 1969): 390–411.

Soudek, Josef. "Aristotle's Theory of Exchange: An Inquiry into the Origin of Economic Analysis." *Proceedings of the American Philosophical Society* 96 (February 1952): 45–75.

Taylor, O. H. "Economics and the Idea of Natural Law." *Quarterly Journal of Economics* 96 (November 1929): 1–39.

Vaughn, Karen I. "John Locke and the Labor Theory of Value." *Journal of Libertarian Studies,* vol. 2, no. 4 (winter, 1978).

Von Leyden, W. "John Locke and Natural Law." *Philosophy* 31 (January 1956): 23–35.

Viano, Carlo Augusto. "I rapporti tra Locke e Shaftesbury e le teorie economiche di Locke." *Rivista di Filosofia* 49 (1958): 69–84.

# INDEX

price, 74–75; and theory of value, 74
Royal Society, 6

Saint Augustine, 116
Scholasticism, 3, 16, 50, 109–10, 116; and interest-taking, 50; and just price, 123–24; and proportionality theory of price, 28; and quantity-value relationship, 20; and theory of value, 17–18
Schumpeter, Joseph, 108–9, 110, 123
Shaftesbury, First Earl of, 8, 10, 11, 12, 16, 77, 111
Smith, Adam, xi, 59–60, 76, 108, 117
Social contract. *See* Government; Labor, theory of; Property, theory of
State of nature: as basis of Locke's economic theories, 50–51, 79; and consent to use money, 93; and distribution of wealth, 51; and economic development, 80–81; and evolution of government, 93–95; and motivation for government, 95–96; and property, 51, 81, 84–85, 91–92; rights under, 80; and "spoilage" limi-

tation, 101; and "sufficiency" limitation, 103–4
Stock, 56
Supply. *See* Quantity

Thomas, David, 8
Trade, balance of. *See* Balance of trade

Value, theory of: antecedents of, 17, 18; as basis for Locke's economic analysis, 17; and labor, 85–86; and money, 31–32; and natural sciences, 28–29. *See also* Money, quantity theory of; Price, proportionality theory of
Vaughan, Rice, 38
Vent: definition of, 25–26; elasticity of, 21–22, 25; and interest, 57; and intrinsic value, 22; and price changes, 22; and quantity theory of money, 36–37; and use value, 22; and velocity of money, 41–42. *See also* Price, proportionality theory of
Vickers, Douglas, ix–x, 64
Von Leyden, W., 4, 5

Wallis, Thomas, 6
Wilkins, John, 6